W9-BNZ-429

AFTER THE SACRIFICE

AFTER THE SACRIFICE

WALTER A. HENRICHSEN

OF THE ZONDERVAN CORPORATION | GRAND RAPIDS, MICHIGAN 49506

AFTER THE SACRIFICE

Grand Rapids, Michigan

Library of Congress Cataloging in Publication Data

Henrichsen, Walter A.
After the sacrifice.

1. Bible. N.T. Hebrews—Commentaries.
I. Title.
BS2775.3.H38 1979 227'.87'077 78-27275
ISBN 0-310-37710-2

Printed in the United States of America.

CONTENTS

FIGURES

INTRODUCTION

Figure 1

THE EPISTLE TO THE HEBREWS

A Comparison of Christ to the Old Testament

Christ: The Fulfillment of the Old Testament Messianic Promises

Christ the Perfect High Priest									Christ the Perfect Way			
He Is Better . . .									A Better Faith . . .			
. . . than Angels		*. . . than Moses*	*. . . Rest*	*. . . than Aaron*	*. . . Assurance*	*. . . Priesthood*	*. . . Covenant*	*. . . Sacrifice*				
The Person and Work of Christ		The Position of Christ	The Provision of Christ	The Perfect Priesthood of Christ	The Promises of Christ	The Perfection of Christ	The Place of Christ's Ministry	The Priestly Ministry of Christ	Endurance of Faith	Explanation & Examples of Faith	Encumbrances of Faith	Expressions of Faith
1:1-14	2:1-18	3:1-19	4:1-16	5:1-14	6:1-20	7:1-28	8:1-13	9:1-10:18	10:19-39	11:1-40	12:1-29	13:1-25
Created the Universe	Redeemed Man	Built the Church	Provided Acceptance	Demonstrated Obedience	Provided a Hope	Intercedes Continuously	Established a Covenant of Grace	Sarificed Himself	Provided a New and Living Way	Gave Promises	Is by Our Side	Is the Same Always
	Heed the Word of God 2:1-4	Don't Be Hardened in Unbelief, 3:12-14			Maturity Affects Assurance 5:11-6:12		**WARNINGS**		Don't Reject Christ, 10:26-31		Heed the Word of God, 12:25-29	

Christ the Perfect High Priest		Christ the Perfect Way
Preeminence of Christ	Preeminence of Christ's Priesthood	Practical Teaching and Exhortation
What do we have?	We have such a High Priest	Having, therefore, let us . . .
Instruction		Exhortation
A New Covenant		An Old Faith
Superior Person	Superior Ministry	Superior Life
What Christ Did — His Person		What We Do — Our Response

INTRODUCTION: APPROACHING THE EPISTLE TO THE HEBREWS

The Epistle to the Hebrews has been called "a rare gem among the King's treasures." And that it is! It is probably the best commentary we have on the Old Testament. Because its writer was inspired by the Holy Spirit, it is an authoritative word from God, and reading it makes it an exciting venture for the Christian. It presents Jesus Christ in His superiority to all there is, and so challenges those who believe in Him to superior living—to that quality of life made possible after the sacrifice of Jesus on the cross.

You may have had the sad experience of reading the Old Testament without understanding either its meaning or its application for today. If so, the Book of Hebrews is for you. With broad and beautiful brush strokes, its writer paints the sweeping design of the Old Testament, interpreting much of its history and explaining many of its prophecies.

It is a mysterious book, some of which is hard to understand. It delves deeply into antiquity, going back to the early days of Israel's existence in the Old Testament. For a better understanding of its teachings, you need to know Israel's Levitical system and you should study the books of Exodus, Leviticus, and Numbers in conjunction with it. The inauguration of the priesthood, the construction of the tabernacle, and the institution of the laws are themes the writer derives from the account of Israel's sojourn at Mount Sinai. It is interesting to note that the temples of Solomon, Zerubbabel, and Herod are not mentioned in the book; only the tabernacle and its related functions are referred to, as though the writer is urging his readers to go back to the very beginning to capture the meaning and significance of the Levitical order.

Part of the mystery of this book is locked up in the uncertainty of who wrote it, why it was written, and when.

The Recipients

We can deduce its original recipients in part from its title, "The Epistle to the Hebrews" (that is, Jews), and in part from the fact that those who read the book initially had to be familiar with the Old Testament.

In Bible times, the term *Jew* was used in much the same way as *Christian* is used in the United States today. The term *Christian* often describes a person who lives a moral, upright life, but who is not necessarily committed to Jesus Christ as Savior and Lord. This kind of Christian knows very little about the Bible. For example, one religious survey asked two questions: "Do you consider yourself a Christian?" and "Can you name the four Gospels?" Most who answered the first question in the affirmative could not answer the second.

A parallel situation existed in the days when the Epistle to the Hebrews was written. The terms *Jew* and *Hebrew* could describe a person's race, religion, or both. Many who were Jews by birth were comparative strangers to what their religion—the Old Testament Scriptures—taught.

The writer of this letter, however, assumed a fairly thorough understanding of the Torah, the five books of Moses, on the part of his readers. This indicates that his recipients were, for the most part, Jews who knew their Scriptures. They were also Christians; the writer frequently makes statements such as: "Even though we speak like this, dear friends, we are confident of better things in your case—things that accompany salvation" (Heb. 6:9).

We also know that they were third-generation Christians. The writer warns, "How shall we escape if we ignore such a great salvation? This salvation, which was first announced by the Lord, was confirmed to us by those who heard him" (Heb. 2:3). The source of the message was Jesus Himself; next, there were "those who heard him," namely the apostles; and the third generation is the writer and the recipients referred to in this passage as "we" and "us."

The Date of Writing

The writer gives us two clues as to when he wrote this letter. The first is contained in his many references to the persecution the church was experiencing. For example, "You sympathized with those in prison and joyfully accepted the confiscation of your property, because you knew that you yourselves had better and lasting possessions" (Heb. 10:34). Around A.D. 64, when Nero was emperor, the Christian church experienced such a persecution. The capital city of Rome had gone up in flames, arson was conjectured, and Nero was suspected by many as being the one who set the city afire for his own ends. To divert attention from himself, the emperor blamed the Christians. He viewed them as members of a subversive secret society, dangerous to the Roman Empire, and therefore an object for persecution and extermination. Many who were arrested were subjected to brutal and humiliating atrocities prior to being killed in cruel and obscene ways.

The second clue is found in the writer's reference to the Jewish sacrificial system. He admonished Hebrew Christians not to continue the ritual of sacrificing animals as a means of obtaining forgiveness of sins (see Heb. 10). These sacrifices were performed only at the temple in Jerusalem. In A.D. 70, the Roman general Titus destroyed Jerusalem and the temple, and animal sacrifices as an integral part of Jewish worship were brought to an end. To this day the Jews have not reinstated them.

Since the writer was addressing Jews who were still sacrificing, the letter to the Hebrews must have been written before A.D. 70. The two internal clues we have, then, lead us to a date somewhere between A.D. 64 (the persecution of Nero) and A.D. 70 (the sack of Jerusalem).

The Author

Who wrote the book poses a more difficult question. Of the many possible candidates, three stand out as the most likely. One is the apostle Paul with his Ph.D. in Judaism. The King James Bible ascribes this book's authorship to him, as do many evangelicals. Then there is Barnabas the Levite. Several of his letters are found among the writings of the early church fathers. The third strong contender is Apollos, of whom it was said that he was "a learned man, with a thorough knowledge of the Scriptures" (Acts 18:24).

Though many have concluded that Paul is the author, the church fathers and many scholars through the centuries have been divided on the issue. As Origen, an early church father, said, "Probably who wrote the epistle in truth God only knows." It's best to leave the authorship problem the way F. F. Bruce does: "In spite of traditional ascriptions and brilliant guesses, its authorship is unknown" *(The Zondervan Pictorial Encyclopedia of the Bible,* III, 87).

The Situation of the Times

To understand the message of the book fully, it is important to appreciate the context in which it was written. In the early years of Christianity, following the death, resurrection and ascension of Christ, the way a person became a Christian was a moot question. It was taken for granted that one came to Christ through the auspices of Judaism. In the minds of the early believers, Judaism and Christianity were not regarded as two separate religions, but one—Christianity being the natural evolution and fulfillment of Judaism. Gentiles did become Christians, but they were Gentiles who had first been converted to Judaism. Luke states that the "God-fearing Jews from every nation in the world" were "Jews and converts to Judaism" (Acts 2:5,10). The Ethiopian eunuch worshiped at the temple in Jerusalem (Acts 8:27), and Cornelius, the Roman centurion, was a God-fearing man (Acts 10:2).

It was not till Paul's ministry got under way that the issue of how a Gentile became a Christian was raised. The essence of the problem was: "Does a Gentile have to come to Christ through Judaism?" or "Can he become a Christian apart from the works of the Law?" This was the much-debated issue at the Jerusalem Council (Acts 15). Living in the 20th century, it is hard for us to imagine the trauma that this question engendered for the first-century Jewish Christians. Many years were to pass before the church realized the implications involved in the fact that Christianity and Judaism were two separate religions.

If Hebrew Christians could not clearly distinguish between Judaism and Christianity, the Romans certainly could. In A.D. 64, after the burning of Rome, Nero began a religious pogrom, with Christians as his target. Christianity became an outlawed religion, and its adherents went underground.

Judaism, however, enjoyed freedom and state protection. Over a century earlier Rome had recognized Judaism as a legal religion of the empire. During the time this letter was written (A.D. 70), Christian Jews were tempted to take shelter under the umbrella provided by the legal, recognized religion of Judaism in order to avoid the savage persecution they would otherwise face. This is understandable (though not necessarily excusable), particularly since at that time there was no sharp distinction between the two religions. "Since in our minds there is no appreciable difference between Christianity and Judaism, during this time of persecution I will call myself a 'Jew,' and then when the 'heat is off,' I'll revert back to Christianity," was in all probability how they thought. This rationalization was made even more tempting since "Jew" refers not only to *religion* but also to *race*. Though they were Christians by religion, they were still Jews by birth.

The writer argued that to hide behind Judaism during this crisis would be tantamount to apostasy. Christianity may have been the natural evolution of Judaism, but the two were by no means the same. The Old Covenant was simply a "shadow" of the New. To return to the Law of Moses after being liberated by the grace of Christ would be as tragic a mistake as that which the people of Israel made at Kadesh Barnea when they rebelled against Moses, refused to enter the Promised Land, and voiced a desire to return to the slavery and oppression guaranteed them in Egypt (Numbers 13–14).

Repeatedly, the writer pleads with his readers not to revert to their old life, but rather to "heed the Word of God."

The Theme and Overview

As the writer makes his forceful and eloquent plea, two parallel themes emerge: *the person and work of Christ* and *the Levitical system of the Old Testament*. The Epistle to the Hebrews compares Jesus Christ to the Old Testament, and sets Him forth as the fulfillment of Old Testament messianic promises.

Figure 1 (page 8) gives an overview of the entire book and divides it into two major sections:

I. Christ the Perfect High Priest, *Hebrews 1:1–10:18*
II. Christ the Perfect Way, *Hebrews 10:19–13:25*

As we compare the themes in this letter, we see that Christ is *better than* all that the Old Testament has to offer. The phrase *better than*, or its equivalent, appears many times in the book.

In chapters 1 and 2, Christ is presented as being better than the angels. Why? Because He is the One who created the world and them, and is the One who has redeemed mankind. The angels are merely messengers of God, but Jesus Christ *is* God.

In chapter 3, Jesus is compared with Moses. Moses led the Israelites out of the bondage of Egypt. Christ redeemed His people from the bondage of sin. Jesus is greater than Moses. Why? Because Moses is part of the church, whereas Jesus *built* the church.

Rest is the point of comparison in chapter 4. Moses tried to provide rest for the Israelites, but because of their unbelief they wandered in the wilderness for forty years. Joshua, as Moses' successor, was finally able to lead them into "the rest of God" when they crossed the Jordan River and entered the Promised Land of Canaan. Centuries later, David said that the rest of God was yet to come (Ps. 95:7,8). What did he mean? To what rest was he referring? That which has now been provided by Jesus Christ. His is a better rest in that it gives His people the assurance and realization of unconditional acceptance in the very presence of God.

Christ is compared with Aaron in chapter 5. Both served in the capacity of God's high priest, but Jesus is better than Aaron. Why? Because Aaron died and his priesthood was temporal. Jesus lives forever and His priesthood is eternal.

In chapter 6, Jesus provides a better assurance. A lack of assurance fosters immaturity, since we become preoccupied with our position in Christ. A clear understanding of His work of redemption lifts us out of the fog of uncertainty and into the bright sunshine of hope. "We have this hope as an anchor of the soul, firm and secure" (Heb. 6:19).

Melchizedek is the subject of chapter 7. Who is this unusual person? The Bible introduces him for the first time when Abraham meets him after rescuing his nephew Lot from the kings of Mesopotamia (see Gen. 14). He is mentioned only once more before the reference in Hebrews in a messianic passage in Psalm 110. Our writer refers to him again and explains who he is. Because Christ's priesthood is after the order of Melchizedek, His is a better priesthood than that of the Levites. The latter is encumbered by the law and so cannot save. Because of who He is, Jesus is "able to save completely those who come to God through him, because He always lives to intercede for them" (Heb. 7:25).

In chapter 8, the writer shows that Christ provides a better covenant than that found in the Old Testament. The law was based on a covenant that was conditional (Exod. 19:6). Jesus' covenant is unconditional (Jer. 31:31-34). The difference between a conditional and an unconditional covenant lies in the preposition *if*. When you see an *if*, you know immediately that the statement is conditional ("if you will do this, then I will do that"). Thc absence of an *if* means that there are no strings attached. In this instance, it means that the covenant established by Jesus is an everlasting covenant of grace.

Jesus provides a better sacrifice. This is the subject of chapters 9:1–10:18. "It is impossible for the blood of bulls and goats to take away sins. . . . Day after day every priest stands and performs his religious duties; again and again he offers the same sacrifices, which can never take away sins. But when this priest had offered for all time one sacrifice for sins, he sat down at the right hand of God" (Heb. 10:4,11-12).

The Old Testament sacrificial system was instituted for two reasons: to show the inadequacies of man's way, and to give a picture of God's way (see Heb. 9:9). God's way, contained in the person of Jesus Christ and His atoning sacrifice for sin, solved the inadequacies of man's way.

The middle of chapter 10 marks a major division in the Epistle (Heb. 10:19). As you glance back at Figure 1 on page 8, you will notice that we now begin the second major section of thc book. The first section dealt with "Christ the Perfect High Priest"; the second deals with "Christ the Perfect Way." In this section, we see that Jesus provides a better faith. To this point, the emphasis has been on *what Christ did*. The thrust of the rest of the book is on *what we do*.

The last part of chapter 10 portrays the "Endurance of Faith" (vv. 19-39). The Hebrew Christians were experiencing hard times, but because of what Jesus did, they could have confidence to enter into His very presence. So the writer urges them not to throw away their confidence (v. 35). By faith we enter into the holiest of all. By faith we endure persecution. By faith we do not cast away our confidence.

The passage in Hebrews 11 unfolds for us the "Explanation and Examples of Faith." After a magnificent definition of faith, we are conducted through God's Hall of Fame and see for ourselves some of the spiritual greats of all time.

In chapter 12, the writer describes the "Encumbrances of Faith." Picture yourself standing in the middle of a great arena. The competition is about to begin, anticipation and tension mount up within you, and as you look up into the crowded stands you see the multitudes cheering you. Some people you recognize; some you don't. A glance toward the sidelines brings reassurance—your coach is there and looks at you confidently and encouragingly.

The race is on! You, the Christian, are competing in the "game of life." Your supporters are the men and women of Hebrews 11. Your coach is the Lord Jesus Christ. He too has run the race that is before you and now stands shouting encouragement, warning you of the pitfalls and hazards, and cheering your gallant efforts.

We conclude with chapter 13—the "Expressions of Faith." Here the writer gives the personal and practical application of faith. He says that faith expresses itself in Christlike interpersonal relations, which implies prior commitment to our Lord and to one another. Christ's example necessitates our expressing our faith in the way we live and in the words we speak.

Interspersed throughout the letter are five warnings and exhortations. The chart on page 8 shows where they occur.

1. Heed the Word of God (2:1-4)
2. Don't Be Hardened in Unbelief (3:12-14)
3. Maturity Affects Assurance (5:11–6:12)
4. Don't Reject Christ (10:26-31)
5. Heed the Word of God (12:25-29)

Notice that the writer ends with the same warning with which he began: "Heed the Word of God." The importance of the Word is one of the underlying themes in the book. He began with the fact that God spoke (Heb. 1:1). By virtue of the fact that it is God who spoke, we had better listen. He later amplified this same theme (Heb. 4:12,13).

In our study of Hebrews we will see the weakness of man contrasted with the person of Christ. Our sinfulness is enough to drive us to despair. But the writer of this letter assures us that if we but trust Jesus Christ, in spite of our sinfulness, all will be well.

Another important truth we will see is the teaching that the Old Testament system of the tabernacle was but a shadow or image of the real, which is in heaven. Our natural inclination is to associate the real with the material—what we can see and feel—and the image with what we cannot experience with our senses. The writer suggests that the opposite is true. The visible is the shadow and the invisible is the real. Heaven is where we find the real tabernacle with the Holy of Holies and our High Priest Jesus. What Moses constructed at the foot of Mount Sinai is only a shadow of the real.

We will also try to unlock some of the mysteries in the book. Why does the writer begin his letter by comparing Christ to angels? What exactly is the rest that God gives? What does the writer mean when he says, "It is impossible for those who have once been enlightened, who have tasted the heavenly gift, who have shared in the Holy Spirit, . . . if they fall away, to be brought back to repentance" (Heb. 6:4,6).

Who is the mysterious Melchizedek? What is the context and meaning of that troublesome passage, "If we deliberately keep on sinning after we have received the knowledge of the truth, no sacrifice for sins is left" (Heb. 10:26)?

Let us embark on our journey through Hebrews as we wait on the Holy Spirit to reveal to us Christ in all His glory, and as we begin to live what may be called "superior living."

OUTLINE OF THE EPISTLE TO THE HEBREWS

I. Christ the Perfect High Priest—*Hebrews 1:1–10:18*
   A. The Person and Work of Christ (1:11–2:18)
      (He Is Better Than the Angels)
      1. Who Christ Is—His Divine Nature (1:1-14)
         a. He is the Revealer of God (vv. 1-3)
         b. He is the Creator of the universe (vv. 4-14)
      2. WARNING No. 1 — Heed the Word of God (2:1-4)
      3. What Christ Did—His Human Nature (2:5-18)
         a. The Incarnation (vv. 5-9)
         b. Glorification (vv. 10-13)
         c. Redemption (vv. 14-18)
   B. The Position of Christ (3:1-19)
      (He Is Better Than Moses)
      1. The Provision—The Faithfulness of God (vv. 1-6)
      2. The Provocation (vv. 7-19)
         a. The failure of Israel (vv. 7-11)
         b. WARNING No. 2 — Don't Be Hardened in Unbelief (vv. 12-14)
         c. Fellowship broken (vv. 15-19)
   C. The Provision of Christ (4:1-16)
      (His Is a Better Rest)

1. God Created (vv. 1-5)
2. Man Realizes (vv. 6-13)
3. Christ Provides (vv. 14-16)

D. The Perfect Priesthood of Christ (5:1-14)
(He Is Better Than Aaron)
1. Obedience Demonstrated (vv. 1-10)
    a. Qualifications of the Old Testament high priest (vv. 1-4)
    b. Qualifications of the perfect sacrifice (vv. 5-10)
2. WARNING No. 3 — Maturity Affects Assurance (Qualifications for Maturity) (vv. 11-14)

E. The Promises of Christ (6:1-20)
(His Is a Better Assurance)
1. WARNING No. 3 (continued) — Maturity Affects Assurance (vv. 1-12)
    a. Failure to mature (from 5:11-14)
    b. Finding assurance (vv. 1-6)
    c. Feelings of assurance (vv. 7-12)
2. Maturity Believes God's Word—Foundation of Assurance (vv. 13-20)

F. The Perfection of Christ (7:1-28)
(His Is a Better Priesthood)
1. His Person (vv. 1-10)
    a. The credentials of Melchizedek (vv. 1-3)
    b. A consideration of Christ's greatness (vv. 4-10)
2. His Promise (vv. 11-22)
    a. Change needed in the old order (vv. 11-19)
    b. The covenant established by an oath (vv. 20-22)
3. His Performance (vv. 23-28)
    a. Contrasting abilities in the priesthoods (vv. 23-25)
    b. Christ's sacrifice of Himself (vv. 26-28)

G. The Place of Christ's Ministry (8:1-13)
(His Is a Better Covenant)
1. A Better Ministry (vv. 1-5)
2. A Better Mediator (v. 6)
3. A Better Covenant (vv. 7-13)

H. The Priestly Ministry of Christ (9:1–10:18)
(His Is a Better Sacrifice)
1. A Better Tabernacle (9:1-12)
    a. The old tabernacle was inadequate (vv. 1-10)

b. Christ the new tabernacle (vv. 11-12)
2. A Better Blood (9:13-28)
a. The necessity of blood (vv. 13-17)
b. To ratify the old covenant (vv. 18-22)
c. To redeem the new covenant (vv. 23-28)
3. A Better Sacrifice (10:1-10)
a. The purpose of the old sacrifices (vv. 1-4)
b. The promised new sacrifice (vv. 5-10)
4. A Better Remission (10:11-18)
a. Forgiveness found in Christ (vv. 11-14)
b. Forgiveness promised in the Old Testament (vv. 15-18)

II. Christ the Perfect Way—*Hebrews 10:19–13:25*
A. Endurance of Faith (10:19-39)
1. Exhortation to Enter (vv. 19-25)
2. WARNING No. 4 — Don't Reject Christ (Exhortation to Fear) (vv. 26-31)
3. Exhortation to Endure (vv. 32-39)
B. Explanation and Examples of Faith (11:1-40)
1. Explanation of Faith (vv. 1-3)
2. Examples of Faith (vv. 4-31)
a. The patriarchs (vv. 4-22)
b. The Exodus and the conquest (vv. 23-31)
3. Exploits of Faith (vv. 32-40)
a. Deliverance from persecution (vv. 32-35a)
b. Deliverance through persecution (vv. 35b-40)
C. Encumbrances of Faith (12:1-29)
1. Race of the Christian (vv. 1,2)
2. Reason for Chastening (vv. 3-11)
3. Response of the Chastened (vv. 12-17)
4. Relationship of Grace (vv. 18-24)
5. WARNING No. 5 — Heed the Word of God (Regard for His Word) (vv. 25-29)
D. Expressions of Faith (13:1-25)
1. Faith Expresses Itself in Virtuous Conduct (vv. 1-6)
2. Faith Expresses Itself in Commitment (vv. 7-16)
3. Faith Expresses Itself in Obedience (vv. 17-25)

Hebrews 1:1 – 2:18

Figure 2

THE PERSON AND WORK OF CHRIST

(He Is Better Than the Angels)

Hebrews 1:1 — 2:18

Who Christ Is — His Divine Nature		WARNING	What Christ Did — His Human Nature		
Revealer	***Creator***		***Incarnation***	***Glorification***	***Redemption***
1:1-3	1:4-14	2:1-4	2:5-9	2:10-13	2:14-18
First Creation		**Heed the Word of God**	Second Creation		
His Work Outside the World			His Work Inside the World		
Son of God			Son of Man		
We Are His Servants			He Is Our Servant		
His Divine Nature: Creator, Sustainer, King, Immutable Conqueror			*His Human Nature*: Suffered, Destroyed, Freed, Made Atonement, Makes Holy, Glorifies, Helps		

1

THE PERSON AND WORK OF CHRIST

The Epistle to the Hebrews compares Jesus Christ to the Old Testament and sets Him forth as the fulfillment of Old Testament messianic prophecies. A theme that threads through the book is "Jesus Christ is better than . . . ." He is better than Moses, better than Aaron, better than the Levitical system of priesthood; He provides a better rest, a better covenant, a better assurance. Jesus Christ is "better than" all!

The first two chapters analyze two aspects of Christ—who He is and what He did—and in so doing compare Him with angels. Jesus Christ is presented as the Revealer, the Creator, the One who was made man, and the One who glorified and redeemed man. In each aspect, He is shown to be superior to angels.

Why does this book open with a comparison of Christ with angels? Why doesn't the writer start by analyzing and demonstrating Christ's superiority to Moses, the Old Testament sacrificial system, or the Levitical priesthood? The reason is that from the outset the writer wanted to make quite clear that his readers knew just who he was talking about: the person of Jesus Christ.

Who Christ Is

He Is the Revealer of God — Hebrews 1:1-3

> [1]In the past God spoke to our forefathers through the prophets at many times and in various ways, [2]but in these last days he has

spoken to us by his Son, whom he appointed heir of all things, and through whom he made the universe. [3]The Son is the radiance of God's glory and the exact representation of his being, sustaining all things by his powerful word. After he had provided purification for sins, he sat down at the right hand of the Majesty in heaven.

From time immemorial, God has sought out His people and communicated with them (see Gen. 3:8-9). Though He was not restricted in His methods, He chose most often to communicate with His people through the medium of the prophet. In our day and age, the word *prophet* evokes a mental picture of a somewhat bedraggled old man with a long white beard speaking in a high-pitched quavering voice. If he were to appear in our neighborhood, he would be an object of pity and, perhaps, mild amusement. This was not so in Old Testament times. The prophet was one who spoke with authority and conviction, uttering the very oracles of God (2 Peter 1:20-21). People would tremble, repent of their wrongdoing, and seek to rectify their ways.

Though the prophets often produced this kind of response, they certainly did not achieve it every time. People didn't always believe them, much less obey their teachings. Prophets were often ridiculed and rejected. Jesus Himself reminds us that many were persecuted, stoned, and killed (Matt. 23:29-38).

God knew how His servants the prophets were treated and how their message was rejected. So whenever He wanted to communicate to His people, or to an individual, in a *decisive* manner, He used an angel as His intermediary. When an angel spoke, people listened. No record is given in the Old Testament of one instance in which an angel was rejected or stoned.

An angel appeared to Abraham and Sarah with the promise of a son, and was believed (Gen. 18). Lot had nocturnal angelic visitors, who warned him of the impending destruction of Sodom and Gomorrah, and he heeded that warning (Gen. 19). Balaam, on his way to spite Israel, came face to face with an angel and ended up blessing the Israelites instead (Num. 22:22–24:9). Throughout the Old Testament, whenever God wanted to communicate *decisively,* He used angels. Gideon was changed from a cowering youth into a valiant man of war on being confronted by "the angel of the Lord" (Judg. 6:11–7:25).

Because of this, the writer of Hebrews wanted to make it clear from the very outset that in Jesus we were not dealing with a mere prophet, nor even with an angel who had come from the very presence of the

Almighty, but with the only Son of God. At various times and in different ways God had spoken to His people through prophets and angels in the past, but "in these last days" He has spoken to us through the medium and in the person of His own Son, our Lord Jesus Christ.

In these last days means the era in which we are living, and the time period in which Jesus Christ is God's final word to us. The angels and prophets of old revealed messages from God to certain individuals or peoples, but Jesus Christ has, once and for all, revealed God to us. He is the brightness of God's glory and the express image of God Himself. When we look at Jesus, we see God face to face. All that God is may be found in Christ. He is the perfect, complete, and exact representation of the Godhead (see Col. 1:15,19; 2:9). He is God's definitive revelation of Himself to mankind.

So Jesus is better than angels. He is as much superior to angels as His name, Son of God, is more illustrious than theirs (ministering spirits, Heb. 1:14). What should our response be to Him? If men bowed in obedience to angels, how much more should we heed and follow the very Son of God.

As we have already noted, there are two parallel themes running through Hebrews as the writer compares and contrasts one with the other. One theme is the person and work of Jesus Christ; the other is the Old Testament system of religion. In this first section, the emphasis is on the first theme—Jesus Christ. But a cursory comparison of Christ to angels is in order before we proceed (see Figure 3).

Figure 3

Jesus Is Better Than Angels Because . . .	
Jesus is . . .	*Angels* are . . .
the Son, 1:5	messengers, 1:7
the One worshiped, 1:6	the ones who worship, 1:6
the Creator, 1:2-10	created beings, 1:7
the Author of salvation, 1:3	ministers of salvation, 1:14
the Ruler, 1:8	subjects, 2:5

Referring to Figure 2 on page 22, we see Christ compared to angels in His divine nature (Heb. 1) and in His human nature (Heb. 2). In this section, we see *who Christ is* and *what He did*. In the first instance, He is the Creator God of the universe, "The express image of [God's] Person." In the second, He is the incarnate Son of God who has redeemed mankind from sin.

He Is the Creator of the Universe — Hebrews 1:4-14

[4]So he became as much superior to the angels as the name he has inherited is superior to theirs.

[5]For to which of the angels did God ever say,

"You are my Son;
today I have become your Father"?

Or again,

"I will be his Father,
and he will be my Son"?

[6]And again, when God brings his firstborn into the world, he says,

"Let all God's angels worship him."

[7]In speaking of the angels he says,

"He makes his angels winds,
his servants flames of fire."

[8]But about the Son he says,

"Your throne, O God, will last for ever and ever,
and righteousness will be the scepter of
your kingdom.
[9]You have loved righteousness and hated wickedness;
therefore, God, your God, has set you
above your companions
by anointing you with the oil of joy."

[10]He also says,

"In the beginning, O Lord, you laid the
foundations of the earth,
and the heavens are the work of your hands.
[11]They will perish, but you remain;
they will all wear out like a garment.
[12]You will roll them up like a robe;
like a garment they will be changed.
But you remain the same,
and your years will never end."

[13]To which of the angels did God ever say,

> "Sit at my right hand
> until I make your enemies your footstool"?

[14]Are not all angels ministering spirits sent to serve those who will inherit salvation?

A number of places in the New Testament acknowledge Jesus Christ as the Creator of the universe. The apostle John recognized Jesus as such when he said, "In the beginning was the Word, and the Word was with God, and the Word was God. He was with God in the beginning. Through him all things were made; without Him nothing was made that has been made. . . . The Word became flesh and lived for a while among us. We have seen his glory, the glory of the one and Only Begotten, who came from the Father, full of grace and truth" (John 1:1-3,14).

Paul, the missionary statesman, said that Jesus

> is the image of the invisible God, the firstborn over all creation. For by him all things were created: things in heaven and on earth, visible and invisible, whether thrones or powers or rulers or authorities; all things were created by him and for him. He is before all things, and in him all things hold together (Col. 1:15-17).

In the Book of Hebrews, the writer reiterates the same truth. He tells us that through Jesus Christ, God made the worlds (Heb. 1:2). Then in verse 10 he ascribes Psalm 102:25 to Jesus, saying, "In the beginning, O Lord, you laid the foundations of the earth, and the heavens are the work of your hands" (Heb. 1:10).

Let us reflect on the implications of this great truth. Science tells us that light travels at the incredible speed of a little over 186,000 miles per second. This means that if you had a rifle capable of shooting a bullet that traveled at the speed of light and was able to follow the curvature of the earth unobstructed, that bullet once fired would pass through your body seven times before you could move out of the way.

Traveling at this stupendous speed, it takes light *four and a half years* to go from the earth to the *nearest* star. Saying it another way, our nearest stellar neighbor is 26,000,000,000,000 miles away. If you and your family counted as fast as you could for the rest of your lives and then added up those numbers you still wouldn't reach 26,000,000,000,000!

This star, four and a half light years away, is our nearest stellar neighbor. Both that star and our own solar system belong to the Milky

Way Galaxy. To cross our galaxy would take 1,000 years, traveling at the speed of light. The Milky Way Galaxy, however, is but one of the countless galaxies in the universe. Our nearest galactic neighbor is the Andromeda Galaxy, and, traveling at 186,000 miles per second, the speed of light, it would take us 2,000,000 years to reach it.

The letter to the Hebrews begins by reminding us that through Jesus Christ all of this was created. It was through Him that God flung the stars into space and brought into existence the uttermost recesses of the universe.

Modern science tells us that, in size, the human being stands about midway in the created order. This means that when compared to man, the atom is as small as the universe is large. That atom, so small that the most powerful microscopes are unable to pick it up, is a solar system all its own with electrons and protons revolving around a nucleus.

The majesty of the Himalayas, the wonder of the mighty Amazon, the beauty of the Norwegian fjords—God created them all through Jesus Christ. Not only was He active in the creation of everything, but He sustains "all things by his powerful word" (Heb. 1:3). Jesus sustains the creation He helped bring into existence. He is the One who maintains order and keeps things under control.

The writer addresses Jesus Christ as God (v. 8). He quotes Psalm 45:6, teaching us that this is a messianic psalm and so refers to Christ. His kingdom—that over which He rules—is eternal (v. 8) and immutable (v. 12).

Not so with the rest of the created order. Here (vv. 10-12) and in other passages, such as 1 Peter 3:10, we are told that the day will come when God will consummate history with the second advent of Christ. In the midst of a creation characterized by change, decay, and ultimate destruction, our Creator, Jesus Christ, is unchanging. This great truth is brought to our attention again when the writer describes Him as "the same yesterday and today and forever" (Heb. 13:8).

Let this vivid picture of the person of Christ remain sharp and clear in your mind as we turn now to a picture of His work on our behalf.

What Christ Did

The Incarnation — Hebrews 2:5-9

> [5]It is not to angels that he has subjected the world to come, about which we are speaking. [6]But there is a place where someone has testified:

> "What is man that you are concerned about him, or the son of man that you should care for him?
> [7]You made him a little lower than the angels; you crowned him with glory and honor [8]and put everything under his feet."
>
> In putting everything under him, God left nothing that is not subject to him. Yet at present we do not see everything subject to him. [9]But we see Jesus, who was made a little lower than the angels, now crowned with glory and honor because he suffered death, so that by the grace of God he might taste death for everyone.

In this paragraph, we see that Jesus Christ became man in order to solve mankind's problem. The writer quotes Psalm 8:4-6 (Heb. 2:6-8), and draws our attention to the problem Christ came to solve. Having made Him a "little lower than the angels," God ordained that man should sit at the apex of His creation on earth.

The entrance of sin, however, changed all of this (see Gen. 3). As the writer says, "Yet at present we do not see everything subject to him" (Heb. 2:8). Man is no longer in control. Afraid of reptiles and wild animals, unable to control the wind and the seas, he is at the mercy of events and circumstances that are beyond him, not the least of which is death itself.

Hence the reason for Jesus' incarnation. It is spelled out clearly for us in verse 9. Jesus became part of the created order. His primary purpose was not to perform miracles and do good deeds, though this was a by-product of His perfect life. His objective was death on the cross— "that by the grace of God he might taste death for everyone" (v. 9). The Christian knows this as the substitutionary death of Christ on his behalf.

I remember once trying to explain this concept to a young man, who was typical of today's generation. He wasn't familiar with the work of Jesus and was struggling to understand the truth of Christ's death for his sins. Suddenly it became clear—as though a light had been turned on in his mind—and he exclaimed, "Oh, you mean Christ took the rap for me!" It wasn't as precise a definition as the theologically acute would like, but he had come to grips with the truth of this verse. Jesus Christ became man to pay the penalty for our sins, that we might have forgiveness and live through Him.

Let's jump over verses 10-13, and look at verses 14-18. In them we see the writer elaborating more fully on what he has just stated.

Redemption — Hebrews 2:14-18

> [14]Since the children have flesh and blood, he too shared in their humanity so that by his death he might destroy him who holds the power of death—that is, the devil— [15]and free those who all their lives were held in slavery by their fear of death. [16]For surely it is not angels he helps, but Abraham's descendants. [17]For this reason he had to be made like his brothers in every way, in order that he might become a merciful and faithful high priest in service to God, and that he might make atonement for the sins of the people. [18]Because he himself suffered when he was tempted, he is able to help those who are being tempted.

These wonderful words explain the process by which our Savior solved the problem of sin and death. Three key words here need to be underlined and examined.

1. *Destroy* (v. 14). By His death Jesus destroyed the works of the devil. When Christ surrendered His life in payment for our sins on that fateful day on Golgotha, Satan's death grip on the human race was broken. Our enemy is a defeated foe.

2. *Free* (v. 15). Death is the fruit of sin. Death is separation, and sin separates. Every man has experienced this in a spiritual sense in that he is separated from God. Dead spiritually, he is hollow and empty inside. His days are numbered and he knows that the experience of physical death is just a matter of time. No one escapes the "grim reaper."

Jesus freed us from this bondage. Charles Wesley, the great hymn writer, put it this way:

> Long my imprisoned spirit lay
> Fast bound in sin and nature's night;
> Thine eye diffused a quickening ray,
> I woke, the dungeon flamed with light;
> My chains fell off, my heart was free,
> I rose, went forth, and followed Thee.

3. *Make atonement* (v. 17). This is a word rich in meaning. The Greek cognate noun is translated "a sacrifice of atonement" (Rom. 3:25) and "atoning sacrifice" (1 John 2:2) and has the meaning of "that sacrifice which makes God righteous in forgiving sin."

Jesus' parable of the tax collector and the Pharisee (Luke 18:9-14) is a familiar story. The two men were praying in the temple. The Pharisee, proud of his position and accomplishments, reminded God of how good he was. In contrast, the tax collector, "would not even look up to heaven, but beat his breast and said, 'God, have mercy on me, a sinner' " (Luke 18:13). The words *have mercy* are the English translation of the Greek word translated "make atonement" here in Hebrews (Heb. 2:17). The tax collector was praying, "Lord, make atonement for me, a sinner—provide for me the sacrifice that will make You righteous in forgiving my sin."

This is what Jesus did for us on the cross, and this is why the Savior says the tax collector "went home justified before God" (Luke 18:14). In His atoning death, Christ reconciled us to God.

That is salvation in three easy-to-understand words. When Jesus tasted death for everyone (Heb. 2:9), He *destroyed* the power of the devil (v. 14), *freed* us from the slavery of the fear of death (v. 15), and *made atonement* for our sins (v. 17).

This is Christ's *past* ministry, which was accomplished when He was here on earth. We also have a brief glimpse of His *present* ministry, now being conducted from heaven (v. 18). Because Jesus suffered the agony of being severely tempted, He is able to help us fight temptation. Jesus used the analogy of a yoke to describe His willingness to help us (Matt. 11:28-30). In this yoke, there is room for two. As we shoulder our burdens, He slides in alongside and helps us carry the load.

What a marvelous ministry! What a wonderful Savior! But there is more. Let us now go back and examine the verses we previously skipped.

Glorification —Hebrews 2:10-13

> [10]In bringing many sons to glory, it was fitting that God, for whom and through whom everything exists, should make the author of their salvation perfect through suffering. [11]Both the one who makes men holy and those who are made holy are of the same family. So Jesus is not ashamed to call them brothers. [12]He says,
>
> "I will declare your name to my brothers;
> in the presence of the congregation I will
> sing your praises."
>
> [13]And again,
>
> "I will put my trust in him."
>
> And again he says,
>
> "Here am I, and the children God has given me."

This passage highlights Christ's *future* ministry. It has to do with "bringing many sons to glory" (v. 10). To support his point to these Jewish Christians, our writer again quotes from the Old Testament, this time drawing our attention to Psalm 22:22 and Isaiah 8:17-18.

The apostle Paul captured this theme for us when he wrote, "Now if we are children, then we are heirs—heirs of God, and co-heirs with Christ, if indeed we share in his sufferings in order that we may also share in his glory. I consider that our present sufferings are not worth comparing with the glory that will be revealed in us" (Rom. 8:17,18). This means that everything that belongs to Jesus Christ belongs to us.

Earlier we saw Jesus as the Creator of this immense universe. Now we are told that we share it with Him. My wife and I enjoy walking through the park at sunset as the last rays of light disappear over the horizon and the stars begin to sprinkle the sky like so many diamonds. It is a real joy to remind ourselves that everything we see in the sky is "our" real estate.

Let's tie this section together by referring once more to Figure 2 on page 22. In chapter 1 we had our attention drawn to the Lord's *first creation,* in chapter 2 to *His second creation*—the creative act of imparting new life in Jesus Christ. *His work outside the world,* that is, His work before He became man, is the subject of chapter 1; chapter 2 discusses *His work inside the world,* that is, the work Jesus did as man. In the first chapter He is portrayed as the *Son of God,* and we see ourselves as His servants; in the second, He is the *Son of Man,* and He serves us by dying on the cross for our sins.

The First Warning

Sandwiched between the first chapter and the main section of chapter 2 is a short paragraph issuing a stern warning.

Heed the Word of God — Hebrews 2:1-4

> [1]We must pay more careful attention, therefore, to what we have heard, so that we do not drift away. [2]For if the message spoken by angels was binding, and every violation and disobedience received its just punishment, [3]how shall we escape if we ignore such a great salvation? This salvation, which was first announced by the Lord, was confirmed to us by those who heard him. [4]God also testified to it by signs, wonders and various miracles, and gifts of the Holy Spirit distributed according to his will.

The Jewish Christians, whom the writer was addressing, knew from their history that to disregard God's Word was pure folly. The angels with whom Jesus is here compared, *always* meant what they said. The writer implies that this message, summarized for us in chapters 1 and 2, came from the Lord Jesus Himself. The logic and application are self-evident: Jesus is better than angels. If history has clearly taught that it is folly to disobey the admonition of angels, how much more the words of the Lord.

By virtue of the first creation, you were born into the world. This is the subject of chapter 1. Through the second creation mentioned in chapter 2, you are born into the family of God. In the first creation, you played a passive role. To be born into God's family, however, you must actively participate by acknowledging your need for the forgiveness of sins and you must receive Jesus Christ into your life.

One of the more obvious applications of the author's warning to heed the Word of God is to acknowledge Jesus Christ as your personal Savior and Lord, and to submit yourself to Him. The Word spoken by the Lord (v. 4) was, "Here I am! I stand at the door and knock. If anyone hears my voice and opens the door, I will go in and eat with him, and he with me" (Rev. 3:20).

If you have never opened the door of your life and invited Jesus Christ in, why not do it right now? There is no better way to begin your study of the Epistle to the Hebrews!

HEBREWS 3:1–19

THE POSITION OF CHRIST
(Better Than That of Moses)
Hebrews 3

Figure 4

The Provision	The Provocation		
Faithfulness of God	Failure of Israel	**Warning**	Fellowship Broken
3:1-6	3:7-11	3:12-14	3:15-19
Christ — Promise, House, Faithful	*Israel* — Unbelief, Wilderness, Rebelled	Don't be hardened in unbelief!	*Us* — ?
Glory to God	Grief to God		
What Christ Did	What We Do		
Exaltation	Exhortation		

2

THE POSITION OF CHRIST

As the Old Testament unfolds, Moses emerges as one of the most prominent figures in Hebrew history. In many respects, he was a national hero lauded by all. He withstood the obstinance of Pharaoh while Israel groveled in servitude. As God's anointed, he delivered Israel from the hand of the oppressor, miraculously bringing that fledgling nation through one impossible situation after another.

At Mount Sinai, Moses mediated between God and man when the latter gave His Law to the people. Through him, the Levitical system was instituted. In terms of work accomplished, he was one of the most impressive men in the annals of Hebrew history.

His counterpart in the New Testament is none other than the Lord Jesus Christ. As the Savior of the world, He delivers God's people from the bondage of sin and the oppressive hand of Satan. He mediates between God and man (1 Tim. 2:5), and as the mediator of a new covenant, He has inaugurated the New Testament system of grace.

We have seen that the Hebrew Christians, addressed by the writer, were facing a time of persecution. Since there was no appreciable difference between Judaism and Christianity in their minds, they were tempted to revert from the outlawed Christian religion to the legal Jewish religion to avoid the otherwise inevitable persecution. Here in chapter 3, the writer is demonstrating that even though there are striking similarities between Christ and Moses, to turn back from Christ to Moses during this time of persecution would be as disastrous a mistake as that committed by Israel at Kadesh Barnea, when in unbelief they turned back on Moses.

The Provision

The theme of the first part of this chapter is: the provision of Christ is better than the provision of Moses. The different sections of the chapter may be seen in the figure on page 36.

The Faithfulness of God — Hebrews 3:1-6

> [1]Therefore, holy brothers, who share in the heavenly calling, fix your thoughts on Jesus, the apostle and high priest whom we confess. [2]He was faithful to the one who appointed him, just as Moses was faithful in all God's house. [3]Jesus has been found worthy of greater honor than Moses, just as the builder of a house has greater honor than the house itself. [4]For every house is built by someone, but God is the builder of everything. [5]Moses was faithful as a servant in all God's house, testifying to what would be said in the future. [6]But Christ is faithful as a son over God's house. And we are his house, if we hold on to our courage and the hope of which we boast.

The key word in this passage is *faithful*. Moses was faithful in all his house, as was Jesus in His house. The Scriptures clearly reveal God's faithfulness in the context of man's failure. God has always been faithful to His people. God was faithful to His people in the Old Testament by sending Moses. He was faithful in the New Testament by sending Jesus Christ.

In this respect, Moses and Christ are similar. Both are expressions of God's faithfulness; both were faithful in executing the will of God (v. 2).

Another point of comparison between Christ and Moses is that both were high priests of God. The function of a high priest is that of a bridge-builder—spanning the gulf that exists between God and man. He is a mediator. A close analogy in today's culture is that of an attorney. His job is to intercede before the judge on behalf of the defendant. Moses functioned as a high priest when he pleaded to God on Israel's behalf on Mount Sinai (Exod. 32:11-14).

He had been on the mountain for forty days and nights and the people thought that he had died. So they urged Aaron to make them a calf of gold, which they worshiped and pronounced as being the god that would lead them back to the land of Egypt. In His anger, God wanted to kill them, but Moses interceded on their behalf. God listened to his plea, and Israel was spared.

This is the present ministry of Jesus Christ before God on behalf of all believers (Heb. 7:25). As man, He underwent the same temptations that all of us have, and so He is eminently qualified to intercede for us. He is an empathetic mediator.

Though the roles and accomplishments of Moses and Christ are similar, some striking differences are apparent as well. These can most easily be seen if we list them side by side (see Figure 5).

Figure 5

CHRIST		MOSES
Built the house	Hebrews 3:3	Part of the house
Is God	Hebrews 3:4	Knew God
A Son	Hebrews 3:5	A servant
Brought them into God's eternal rest (Hebrews 4:10)		Brought them to the border of God's temporal rest (Hebrews 3:10)

"Jesus has been found worthy of greater honor than Moses, just as the builder of a house has greater honor than the house itself" (Heb. 3:3). Christ built the house, in which Moses was but a part.

The word *house* can be used in two senses. It is usually used in reference to a dwelling place, but it can also refer to a family. For example, in British history, we read about families such as "the house of York," "the house of Tudor," and "the house of Stuart."

Our use of *church* is another example. By it we can mean the building on the corner of Sixth and Elm, a particular congregation, a denomination, or the universal family of God.

House as a reference to a family unit is familiar in the Old Testament. During the period of the divided kingdom, the Hebrew nation consisted of "the house of Israel" (the northern tribes) and "the house of Judah" (the southern tribes).

Here the writer is not using *house* to refer to a building made of stone, but to God's family—the body of Christ. Moses was part of

God's house as a servant (v. 5). Christ is ruler over God's house as a Son. Christ is better than Moses.

In summary, we can see that God has always been faithful to His people. Moses was such an expression in the Old Testament; Jesus Christ, a similar expression in the New Testament. Jesus, however, is better than Moses in that when God expressed His faithfulness in the Old Testament, it was in the person of His servant, while in the New Testament it was in the person of His Son.

The Provocation

The Failure of Israel — Hebrews 3:7-11

[7]So, as the Holy Spirit says:

"Today, if you hear his voice,
[8] do not harden your hearts
as you did in the rebellion,
during the time of testing in the desert,
[9]where your fathers tested and tried me,
and for forty years saw what I did.
[10]That is why I was angry with that generation,
and I said, 'Their hearts are always going astray,
and they have not known my ways.'
[11]So I declared on oath in my anger,
'They shall never enter my rest.'"

At verse 7, the writer shifts his argument. Because Jesus is better than Moses, to turn back *to* Moses at this time of persecution would be as tragic a mistake as Israel made when that nation turned back *on* Moses at Kadesh Barnea.

The incident is described in Numbers 13–14. The journey of the Israelites through the wilderness was coming to a close. The crossing of the Red Sea, the receiving of the Ten Commandments at Mount Sinai, and the construction of the tabernacle were now all behind them. After an arduous two-year trek, the people of Israel found themselves on the outskirts of the Promised Land at an encampment called Kadesh Barnea.

Here Moses ordered Israel to pitch camp. A reconnaissance team was picked—one man from each of the 12 tribes—and sent in to "spy out the land of Canaan," assess the enemy position, and report back to the waiting Israelite army.

They did this, but the report of the majority filled the hearts of the people with fear. They reported to Moses: "'We went into the land to which you sent us, and it does flow with milk and honey! Here is its fruit. But the people who live there are powerful, and the cities are fortified and very large. We even saw descendants of Anak there. The Amalekites live in Negev; the Hittites, Jebusites and Amorites live in the hill country; and the Canaanites live near the sea and along the Jordan.' Then Caleb silenced the people before Moses and said, 'We should go up and take possession of the land, for we can certainly do it.' " (Num. 13:27-30). True, it was a fruitful land, one flowing with "milk and honey." But they had encountered the unexpected giants. These sons of Anak were just too much. There was no way Israel could defeat them.

Two members of the team brought a minority report. "Sure it's going to be difficult, but with God's help, we can do it." But it was too late. The damage had been done. Panic had already gripped the people, and there was no way they could be persuaded to go forward. Reason gave way to fear. It was one of the most tragic episodes in Israel's history. Since they turned their backs on God's promises, He had to punish them and they spent the next forty years wandering in the wilderness.

A generation later Moses wrote that it took eleven days to go from Horeb to Kadesh Barnea by the Mount Seir road (Deut. 1:2). Because they took counsel with their fears rather than God's promises, this eleven-day journey was prolonged by forty years. In a word, Israel's problem was unbelief. God had made them a promise when He said, "I will give you this land." But they put more stock in the giants' abilities than in God's willingness to fulfill His promise.

It took the people of Israel forty years to make an eleven-day journey because they had not learned an important lesson. A whole generation was wasted. In this passage, the writer pleads with us to learn from Israel's mistake vicariously rather than blunder into the same tragic pattern of unbelief.

Unbelief was Israel's problem, and without constant vigilance it can be ours too. We are foolish if we think we are smarter or more spiritual than Israel. God has given us promises just as He gave them to His Old Testament people. Refusing to act on God's promises because of unbelief can cause an individual to squander his life in the wilderness of mediocrity.

At Kadesh Barnea, God was using the giants in order to *test* Israel (Heb. 3:8). God allowed them to meet the "sons of Anak" so they could fall back on His promises rather than rely on their own strength and ability. Then Israel tempted or tested God by responding to unfavorable circumstances with doubt and anxiety (v. 9).

When God tests us, it is because He has our best interest at heart. When we test God, it is because we have our best interest at heart. Let this truth sink in: God tests us because He loves us and wants our faith to grow in strength and maturity; we test God because we love ourselves. In both cases, "our best interest" is the motive behind the testing.

From what source, then, does the conflict of interest come? In deciding who best knows what we need. It is precisely at this point that unbelief enters the picture. In essence, what Israel said was, "We agree that our best interest should be the prime consideration but disagree as to how it can best be served. We can hardly believe that fighting giants is in our best interest, so we refuse to enter the Promised Land." *Unbelief is believing that what I think is my best interest surpasses what God thinks is my best interest.*

How can we apply this truth? Suppose the Lord wants your son or daughter on the mission field. Your concept of such an assignment is at best that your child will live in obscurity, and at worst that he will undergo suffering, want, hardship, and disease. You don't mind giving your finances to the cause of Christ, but your children? That is another thing. So you reason with God, "Lord, I want my child to serve You, and with this in mind I have given him the best education that money can buy. It just seems to me that for my son to go overseas would be a waste of his talents. Now let me tell You where I think he can best serve You. . . ."

Often in life we come face to face with "giants." We meet them when our business folds, our spouse dies, our child goes on drugs, or in a myriad of other situations. In the throes of these seemingly adverse circumstances, we are tempted to think, *How can this possibly be of benefit to me?* It could be that God is testing us. We can either rebel and in anger turn back on God, or we can learn from Israel's mistake and with the eyes of faith meet those giants, convinced that God will undertake for us and make us better people in the process.

In summarizing the first two sections of Hebrews 3, let us refer again to Figure 4 on page 36. In the first section, glory was given to God through the lives of Moses and Christ; in the second, grief was given to God through Israel's unbelief. In verses 1-6, we see what Christ did; in verses 7-11, we see what we will do unless we learn from Israel's mistake. In the first section, God is exalted; in the second, we are exhorted not to miss God's wonderful plan for our lives.

Before examining the warning in verses 12-14, let us see what verses 15-19 have to say to us.

Fellowship Broken — Hebrews 3:15-19

[15]As has just been said:

> "Today, if you hear his voice,
> do not harden your hearts
> as you did in the rebellion."

[16]Who were they who heard and rebelled? Were they not all those Moses led out of Egypt? [17]And with whom was he angry for forty years? Was it not with those who sinned, whose bodies fell in the desert? [18]And to whom did God swear that they would never enter his rest if not to those who disobeyed? [19]So we see that they were not able to enter, because of their unbelief.

Two parallel thoughts thread their way through this passage: what Israel did, and what God did in response to Israel's unbelief.

What Israel Did

They heard (v. 16). It wasn't that Israel did not understand what God expected of them. God had spoken clearly to the people. Israel's problem was volitional, not intellectual.

They sinned (v. 17). Their response to God's instructions was overt rebellion. They thought they knew what was best for them better than God did.

They did not believe (v. 19). Panic struck the camp like a plague. Everywhere they looked, the Israelites thought they saw giants. In front of them and behind them. Even when they closed their eyes, all they saw were giants. Defeat was imminent and inevitable. If you had asked them if they believed God *could* kill giants, they no doubt would have answered with a resounding "yes." The people of Israel believed God *could* kill giants. It was just that they did not believe He *would*.

In most instances, unbelief does not question God's ability to do something, but His willingness to do it. Will He do what He says He will do?

What God Did

He was provoked (v. 16). If you want to make God angry, tell Him you think He is a liar. In effect, that's what Israel did: they rebelled. Such an attitude is just as sure to break your fellowship with God as it would with another person. Yet many are guilty of such heresy almost daily.

God says, "My grace is sufficient for you" (2 Cor. 12:9), yet we often respond to trials and difficulties with weakness. God says, "Do not be anxious about anything" (Phil. 4:6), yet we fret over the least uncertainty. God says, "I will always make you rich enough to be generous" (2 Cor. 9:11 NEB), yet we hoard our finances as though such a promise did not exist. "God is not a man, that he should lie, nor a son of man, that he should change his mind. Does he speak and not act? Does he promise and not fulfill?" (Num. 23:19)

He was grieved (v. 17). Displeased with their behavior, God lamented the fact that He ever brought them out of Egypt. So keenly did God feel this that the writer says His anger lasted forty years.

He swore vengeance (v. 18). God revoked his former promise and made a new one. He vowed that the rebellious generation would not enter Canaan but would turn back and live as vagrants in the wilderness. God based His promise on two requests made by Israel.

The first was the statement of the people: "If only we had died in Egypt! Or in this desert!" (Num. 14:2). In response God said, "You wish to die in the wilderness! Let it be so then. You will wander in the wilderness till you die."

The second request was: "Why is the Lord bringing us to this land only to let us fall by the sword? Our wives and children will be taken as plunder. Wouldn't it be better for us to go back to Egypt?" (Num. 14:3). Next to this verse in my Bible I have written, "One of the first signs of unbelief is an undue concern for wife and children." Men frightened of giants are hiding behind their wives and children.

In essence, God gave them exactly what they asked for. They wanted to die in the wilderness and God gave them their wish. They were afraid of what might happen to their children, so God said He would assume responsibility for them. The psalmist's commentary on the incident was, "But they soon forgot what he had done and did not wait for his counsel. In the desert they gave in to their craving; in the wasteland they put God to the test. So he gave them what they asked for, but sent a wasting disease upon them." (Ps. 106:13-15). Of this, Amy Carmichael said, "Be careful what you set your heart on, for surely it will be yours." You can experience no worse fate in life than to get what you want when what you want is not the same as the perfect will of God.

The Second Warning
Don't Be Hardened in Unbelief—Hebrews 3:12-14

> [12]See to it, brothers, that none of you has a sinful, unbelieving heart that turns away from the living God. [13]But encourage one another daily, as long as it is called Today, so that none of you may be hardened by sin's deceitfulness. [14]We have come to share in Christ if we hold firmly till the end the confidence we had at first.

Do you see yourself in what Israel experienced in the wilderness? Is your life drab and cloaked with mediocrity? Maybe you have heard of the abundant life but have no idea what it means. Like Israel, you have been wandering in the wilderness of life.

We are urged to encourage one another (v. 13) so that we may share in Christ's blessing (v. 14).

Two things are necessary: We must trust Him and we must obey Him. Trust precedes obedience. Is God's Word trustworthy? Do you really believe He will do what He has promised? If so, you must obey Him. Trust without obedience is only half the equation. It is like being told by your physician that you can be cured, but only if you do what you are asked to do. You will never partake in Christ's blessing till you *act* on His promises. Figure 4 on page 36 brings this into focus.

God gave a promise. Israel responded in unbelief.

God provided a house. Israel responded by choosing the wilderness.

God was faithful. Israel responded in rebellion.

How we respond to God is our decision. Two avenues are open to us: we can follow the example of Israel, respond in unbelief, and squander our lives in the wilderness of mediocrity. Or we can follow the example of Jesus Christ (Heb. 5:8).

The large question mark on the chart is there for a reason. As with Moses and Jesus, so God has called *you* to a life of faithfulness. He has called *you* to mediate between Himself and your fellowmen through evangelism and prayer. Our Lord has asked *you* to lead your neighbors and friends out of captivity and bondage into a wonderful relationship with Jesus Christ. You can follow the example of Christ or the example of Israel. The choice is yours.

HEBREWS 4:1–16

Figure 6

THE PROVISION OF CHRIST

(His Is a Better Rest)

Hebrews 4

Faith vs. Unbelief

God Created		Man Realizes			Christ Provides		
					Because of Christ's . . .		
Opportunity	Rest	The Rest Is Timeless	Requirements for Rest	Exposure by the Word	*. . . Propitiation* Mediation	*. . . Incarnation* Empathy	*. . . Glorification* Access
4:1-2	4:3-5	4:6-9	4:10-11	4:12-13	4:14	4:15	4:16

Past Rest	Present Rest	
Explained	Encouraged	Entered
God's Work Completed	Our Works Cease	Christ's Work Continues
Spoken Word Promises	Written Word Reveals	Incarnate Word Accepts
Let Us Be Careful	Let Us Make Every Effort	Let Us Approach

3

THE PROVISION OF CHRIST

To the weary, rest is a delightful reprieve.

God created heaven and earth in six days and rested on the seventh. In doing so, He established a pattern for man, for we are told, "Six days you shall labor and do all your work, but the seventh day is a day of rest to the Lord your God. In it you shall not do any work" (Exod. 20:9-10). So the concept of rest has been with us since creation.

In the preceding section, we were told that Israel failed to enter God's rest because of unbelief. When God's rest was denied them because of their sin, two things happened: their fellowship with God was broken and they missed God's perfect will for their lives.

In all interpersonal relationships, unbelief causes broken fellowship. If you make a promise to your friend and he says, "I don't believe you," it is difficult to have a good friendship from then on. Likewise, when at Kadesh Barnea God said He would assume responsibility for their safe entry into Canaan, and Israel responded by questioning His veracity, fellowship was broken. The verdict God gave was: "For forty years—one year for each of the forty days you explored the land—you will suffer for your sins and know what it is like to have me against you" (Num. 14:34). The people of Israel were denied God's rest because they had thwarted God's plan. "So we see that they were not able to enter, because of their unbelief" (Heb. 3:19).

To enter God's rest is to live in unbroken fellowship with Him. Rest in this context refers to fellowship, not salvation. *Broken fellowship, not a loss of salvation, was what Israel experienced at Kadesh Barnea.*

Granted, all of the Israelites "twenty years old or more" died in the wilderness, except Joshua and Caleb. But this does not mean that in death they experienced eternal separation from God. Aaron, Miriam, Moses, and many others died and were buried east of Jordan, but this does not mean they were eternally lost. Crossing Jordan is not analogous to entering heaven, but to restoring broken fellowship.

Unbelief destroyed fellowship when Israel failed to believe the promises of God. Note the link between God's promises and God's rest, "Therefore, since the promise of entering his rest still stands, let us be careful that none of you be found to have fallen short of it" (Heb. 4:1). Acting on the promises of God is foundational to entering the rest of God. What was true for ancient Israel is also true for us today.

Three times in this section the writer stirs us into action with the little phrase "let us." "Let us be careful" (v. 1), "let us make every effort" (v. 11), and "let us approach" (v. 16). These three commands accent the chapter divisions (See Figure 6 on page 48).

- God created, therefore let us be careful (Heb. 4:1-5).
- Man realizes, therefore let us make every effort (Heb. 4:6-13).
- Christ provides, therefore let us approach (Heb. 4:14-16).

God created both the rest and the opportunity to enter His rest. In order to participate in God's rest, man must realize that the rest is timeless, that there are certain requirements he must meet, and that God sees him the way he is.

Even though man is exposed in all his sinfulness before God, Christ provides mediation, empathy, and access into the very presence of the Lord.

God created — *Hebrews 4:1-5*

[1]Therefore, since the promise of entering his rest still stands, let us be careful that none of you be found to have fallen short of it. [2]For we also have had the gospel preached to us, just as they did; but the message they heard was of no value to them, because those who heard it did not combine it with faith. [3]Now we who have believed enter that rest, just as God has said,

"So I declared on oath in my anger,

> 'They shall never enter my rest.'"
>
> And yet his work has been finished since the creation of the world. [4]For somewhere he has spoken about the seventh day in these words: "And on the seventh day God rested from all his work." [5]And again in the passage above he says, "They shall never enter my rest."

Opportunity — Hebrews 4:1-2

In this passage, we see that God created an opportunity to enter His rest by assuming responsibility for getting the Word out. "To us, just as they did" indicates that just as Israel heard the Gospel, so have we (see Heb. 3:16).

We are admonished to "be careful" (v. 1) because of the Israelites' example. When they heard God's promises, they did not add the necessary ingredient of faith. God's promises were given to them in vain.

God says to us today, "I have done My part. I have given you promises just as I gave My people during the Exodus. Now it is up to you. You must respond to them in faith by acting on them."

God has done His part in creating an opportunity to enter His rest by propagating the Good News. Let us be careful lest we fail to do our part.

The writer is trying to communicate the idea of motivating you to give your all. It is a being careful that brings into focus the issues and causes you to act on what you know to be right regardless of the price. This is the only response God desires from those who have been given His promises.

As you come to the end of your days, few things in life could be worse than realizing that you made the tragic mistake of missing the opportunity that God had provided for you. Instead of involving yourself in the exciting promises of God, you find that you gave yourself to the wrong things and consequently wandered for forty years in the wilderness of mediocrity.

Rest — Hebrews 4:3-5

This passage uses the word *rest* in three senses. These are summarized in Figure 7, page 52.

Creation Rest

1. At creation God provided a rest for His people. Israel did not enter Canaan, which was an expression of His rest, but we are promised that we can enter the rest that has been provided.

Figure 7

Creation Rest	Canaan Rest	Continued Rest
Provided at creation	They did not enter	We can
Rest was completed	Physical	Spiritual
God finished the work	They felt they had to do more	We must not
Promised	Unbelief	Faith

2. Provision for our rest was completed at creation. For Israel, it had the physical manifestation of the Promised Land, which was the fulfillment of God's promise to them. For us, God's rest takes on a spiritual dimension in that it encompasses fellowship with Him.

3. God finished the work. Victory over the giants was God's responsibility. The Israelites were to possess the land, and did so forty years later under the leadership of Joshua. But Israel took too much on themselves at Kadesh Barnea and assumed that they, not God, would have to defeat the giants. Learning from Israel's mistake, we must remember that fellowship with God on a day-by-day basis is possible because of what God has done. We are simply to believe His promises.

4. At creation God promised the existence of a rest. Israel responded in unbelief when they were at Canaan's borders. We must believe God's promises and respond in faith rather than imitate Israel.

Canaan Rest

The rest God provided for Israel at Canaan was the subject of chapter 3. Here the writer examines more closely the creation rest (Heb. 4:3-5).

All of God's work was completed from before the foundation of the world. History is merely an unfolding of what God accomplished at the beginning. So "on the seventh day God rested from all his work" (Heb. 4:4).

An obvious illustration of this is the Canaan rest referred to in Numbers 13–14 and discussed in Hebrews 3. God's rest for Israel was provided from the world's foundation. That is why they had nothing to worry about. It was a completed work. All they had to do was believe God and possess the land.

But Israel didn't quite see it that way. To them it was a future work, dependent on their ability to kill giants. This is why their courage evaporated and their hearts melted with fear.

Continued Rest

Our application is likewise apparent. People are sometimes heard to say, "Back in the Old Testament, God seemed to be at work in a fantastic way. He performed miracles on behalf of His people. Wouldn't it be wonderful if He were at work today as He was then?" The writer assures us that God is as active today as He has ever been. He is still unfolding history and revealing His perfect plan.

Notice what Moses records about creation. Each of the six creation days ends with the phrase "and there was evening, and there was morning—the ——— day" (Gen. 1:5,8,13,19,23,31). Then God "rested on the seventh day from all His work" (Gen. 2:2-3). No mention is made of there being an evening at the end of the seventh day. Jewish rabbinical tradition says the evening is not mentioned because God's rest continues forever. Since God's rest was completed at creation when He had finished His work, it is a perpetual rest. This is why "there remains, then, a Sabbath-rest for the people of God" (Heb. 4:9).

The writer uses the creation rest to draw our attention to the fact that God's rest is available for all people in all ages. He uses the Canaan rest to point out that failure to enter God's rest is the result of unbelief and that we should learn from Israel.

You too can have that rest. God has a place for you in the work He finished at creation. All you need to do is believe what He says and act accordingly.

Man Realizes — *Hebrews 4:6-13*

[6]It still remains that some will enter that rest, and those who formerly had the gospel preached to them did not go in, because of their disobedience. [7]Therefore God again set a certain day, calling it Today, when a long time later he spoke through David, as was said before:

> "Today, if you hear his voice,
> do not harden your hearts."

[8]For if Joshua had given them rest, God would not have spoken

later about another day. [9]There remains, then, a Sabbath-rest for the people of God; [10]for anyone who enters God's rest also rests from his own work, just as God did from his. [11]Let us, therefore, make every effort to enter that rest, so that no one will fall by following their example of disobedience.

[12]The word of God is living and active. Sharper than any double-edged sword, it penetrates even to dividing soul and spirit, joints and marrow; it judges the thoughts and attitudes of the heart. [13]Nothing in all creation is hidden from God's sight. Everything is uncovered and laid bare before the eyes of him to whom we must give account.

The Rest Is Timeless — Hebrews 4:6-9

If he is ever to enter God's rest, man must realize that it is timeless. To prove his point, the writer quotes from Psalm 95:7, 8, in which David refers to God's rest (v. 7). Remember that after the Israelites' forty years of wandering in the wilderness, Joshua led them across the Jordan River into the Promised Land, which was representative of the rest of God.

The writer argues that if Joshua had provided the people with the *only* rest God had in mind, David, years later, would not have referred to yet another rest. (Remember also that *Jesus* is the New Testament Greek rendering of the Old Testament name *Joshua*, thus *Jesus* is used for the word *Joshua* in the KJV.) So the writer concludes, "There remains, then, a Sabbath-rest for the people of God" (v. 9). God's rest is available to all people in all ages who seek to enter by faith.

Requirements for Rest — Hebrews 4:10, 11

This passage seems to be a contradiction. First the writer says, "Rests from his own work" (v. 10), then he exhorts, "Let us . . . make every effort" (v. 11). In reality, the seemingly contradictory ideas are the requirements for entering into God's rest. In some respects, they are simply a review of what we learned earlier (Heb. 3).

To rest from our own work is discussed later on, where our works are referred to as "dead works" (KJV), the works of self-effort (Heb. 6:1). They falsely imply that our relationship with God can be the fruit of self-effort. But ours is a grace relationship with God—not a works relationship. It has always been so, and always will be.

The effort referred to here is the effort of faith (v. 11). It is hard to believe the promises of God. Why? Because they appear too good to be true. God says all we have to do is *confess* our sins to be forgiven (1 John 1:9). It is hard for us to forgive ourselves, much less to comprehend that we can be forgiven by a perfect God. God says we are to seek His kingdom, and He will assume responsibility for all our needs (Matt. 6:33). It is hard for us to believe that our daily needs do not have to be our number-one priority. We have to work at believing God.

The battle is the Lord's, but we must take up our swords. Giants must be killed; they do not drop dead by themselves. But the questions we must ask are these: "Whose battle is it? In whose strength do we fight?" If we believe the sword is an expression of the fact that the battle is ours, we will run from the giants. If we believe that though we have to fight, the battle is the Lord's, then we will claim His promise, attack in faith, and defeat the giants.

This distinction is clearly seen in how David and Saul viewed Goliath. Saul took one look at Goliath and said, "He is so big, I can't hit him!" David's response, however, was, "He is so big, I can't miss!" One saw Goliath through the eyes of unbelief, the other through the eyes of faith. Saul saw the battle as being his own—and he panicked. David saw the battle as being the Lord's—and he attacked and prevailed.

Exposure by the Word — Hebrews 4:12-13

These are strange words penned in the middle of an explanation of God's rest. Most Christians are familiar with them, but why are they in this context? How do they fit?

Suppose I were able to read every thought that ever passed through your mind. What would you feel like in my presence? Quite uncomfortable, I imagine. I know that if I thought you could see me as I really am, I would do my utmost to avoid you.

This is precisely what this passage tells us God is able to do. Our thought lives are completely unveiled to Him. God sees us just the way we are.

Now the context of these verses is dealing with abiding in God's presence on a day-by-day basis in unbroken fellowship. If I seek to avoid the presence of anyone who can see me the way I am in all my sinfulness, why don't I apply this to God—especially since I know that He is also my Judge? In short, why would I *want* to enter His rest? Wouldn't I rather seek to avoid His presence?

The answers to these questions are found in seeing what Christ has already provided.

Christ Provides — *Hebrews 4:14-16*

> [14]Therefore, since we have a great high priest who has gone into heaven, Jesus the Son of God, let us hold firmly to the faith we profess. [15]For we do not have a high priest who is unable to sympathize with our weaknesses, but we have one who has been tempted in every way, just as we are—yet was without sin. [16]Let us then approach the throne of grace with confidence, so that we may receive mercy and find grace to help us in our time of need.

Our acceptance by God is not based on insufficient evidence. As His children, we are promised forgiveness of sins, unconditional love, and acceptance—all these in spite of the fact that God knows us more intimately than any human being on the face of the earth, including ourselves.

In your interpersonal relationships with those you love and enjoy, have you ever wondered if they would accept you if they knew what you *really* were? We can know that Jesus totally accepts us the way we are, even though He knows what we are really like. This is an example of what we have been taught earlier (v. 11). To believe that God accepts us after seeing us in the nakedness of our innermost thoughts definitely requires the labor of faith.

We are given three reasons why we can enter God's rest even though we are exposed before Him by His Word.

Mediation — Hebrews 4:14

Our great High Priest, Jesus Christ, is in heaven mediating between God and us. He is our defense attorney standing before the judgment seat of God. Our violation of God's commands is brought before the court and the verdict is returned: "Guilty as charged!" Then Jesus Christ asks for our acquittal on the basis of His having already paid the penalty. God as the Judge rules that our guilt is to be placed on Jesus and that we are to be set free.

All this takes place on our behalf when we receive Christ as our Savior and Lord. Even as God's children, however, we continue to slip back into sin and unbelief, but Jesus, our "defense lawyer," continues to plead our cause day and night before God. This is why we do not have to shrink back from entering God's rest.

Empathy — Hebrews 4:15

Not only does our Savior function as our great High Priest, but He "has been tempted in every way, just as we are—yet was without sin." The Bible never exaggerates. He was in *every* way tempted as we are. We have not experienced and never will experience a temptation that Jesus Christ has not Himself undergone.

Jesus accepts us because He knows what we are going through. He is also able to help us resist temptation because, though He was tempted as we are, He never sinned. He knows the path to victory and can confidently lead us along the way.

Access — Hebrews 4:16

The picture painted for us in this passage is one of an ancient throne room. In the Near Eastern empires during Bible times, only one person was allowed to enter the presence of the king uninvited—his firstborn son, the heir to the throne. Even the queen could not enter her husband's presence without first receiving an invitation.

This is graphically illustrated in a scene from the Book of Esther. Mordecai asked his cousin Esther to go before her husband, the king and intercede on behalf of the Jews. Willing to go, she asked for prayer because she knew that if the king did not hold out his golden sceptre to her as a demonstration of his acceptance of her coming before him, she would be sentenced to death.

Here the writer suggests that we have the same rights as the king's firstborn son and heir to the throne. The King of Kings and Lord of Lords has extended to us the same privileges that His own Son has. Coming into God's very presence, we can obtain mercy for our wrongdoing and a generous portion of His grace during times of need.

In summary, referring to the chart on page 48, it is easy to see how the three paragraphs in the chapter relate to one another. In the first section, God's rest is *explained* to us; we are then *encouraged* to learn that He has a rest for us too; finally, we see that this rest can be *entered* because of what Jesus did, is doing, and will continue to do for us. Because of Christ's *propitiation,* He is our *mediator;* because of His *incarnation,* He is *empathetic;* because of His *glorification,* we have *access* into God's presence.

In the first paragraph, we discover *God's work is completed* at creation; in the next paragraph, we see that *our works cease* at conversion; in the last paragraph, we notice that *Christ's work continues* in the presence of God.

The first paragraph emphasizes that the *spoken Word promises* us God's rest; the thrust of the second paragraph is that the *written Word reveals* our sins; the last paragraph shows that Jesus, the *incarnate Word, accepts* us just the way we are.

It takes a great deal of faith to believe that God accepts us the way we are. He does not accept us for the way we would like to be, or for the way we feel He would like us to be. He accepts us just as we are.

Acceptance by God necessitates self-acceptance, and that is hard. To accept myself for the way I am is difficult because I know what I am like, and I often make myself sick! But I must accept myself because God accepts me, and I dare not establish a standard of acceptance higher than God's.

God's acceptance of us also forces us to accept one another. Because God accepts you, I also must accept you, and, similarly, you must accept me. I must not make my standard of acceptance higher than God's standard. To do this would be to declare myself more righteous than God.

Self-acceptance and acceptance of others is therefore built on the foundation of God's acceptance of us. It is right here that we should "be careful that none of [us] be found to have fallen short of it" (Heb. 4:1). It is so hard to believe that God, knowing us the way He does, can really accept us. But He promises that He does. We can take Him at His Word and enter His rest, or we can, by default, follow Israel into the wilderness.

HEBREWS 5:1–14

Figure 8

THE PERFECT PRIESTHOOD OF CHRIST

(Better Than That of Aaron)

Hebrews 5

Obedience Demonstrated		Obedience Desired
Qualifications of the Old Testament High Priest	Qualifications of the Perfect Sacrifice	Qualifications for Maturity
5:1-4	5:5-10	5:11-14
Requirements	Requirements Met	**WARNING!**
Temporal	Eternal	
Offered Animals	Offered Himself	The Christian Who Refuses to Grow Up
Aaron	Christ	Believer
Appointed From Men	Author of Salvation	Application of the Word

4

THE PERFECT PRIESTHOOD OF CHRIST

Faced with the question of how God's people enter His rest, the writer introduces the high priestly ministry of Jesus Christ into the equation. "Therefore, since we have a great high priest who has gone into heaven, Jesus the Son of God . . ." (Heb. 4:14).

The remainder of the first part of this letter contains a vivid description of what Jesus' high priestly work entails (Heb. 4:14–10:18). His qualifications as High Priest is the subject of this section, and may be divided into three paragraphs (see Figure 8 on page 60):

- Qualifications of the Old Testament High Priest (5:1-4)
- Qualifications of the Perfect Sacrifice (5:5-10)
- Qualifications for Maturity (5:11-14)

In the first two paragraphs, Jesus' obedience to the Father is demonstrated. The last paragraph contains the third of five warnings in the Book of Hebrews. In this warning we see that *our* obedience to the Father is desired.

Qualifications of the Old Testament High Priest—*Hebrews 5:1-4*

[1]Every high priest is selected from among men and is appointed to represent them in matters related to God, to offer gifts and sacrifices for sins. [2]He is able to deal gently with those who are ignorant and are going astray, since he himself is subject to weakness. [3]This is why he has to offer sacrifices for his own sins, as well as for the sins of the people.

[4]No one takes this honor upon himself; he must be called by God, just as Aaron was.

The position of high priest was a sacred office in the Hebrew faith, as it is in any system of worship. A person could not succeed to this office merely at whim, for certain qualifications for the high priesthood had been clearly given in Scripture. Likewise, it was important in the ministry of Jesus that He meet all the Law's requirements. He Himself said, "Do not think that I have come to abolish the Law or the Prophets; I have not come to abolish them but to fulfill them" (Matt. 5:17). The prerequisites for the high priesthood are listed in this passage. Using them, we can compare Christ with the Levitical priesthood.

Before we examine these likenesses and differences, we would do well to remind ourselves that no one, at any time, has ever been able to enter the presence of God without the mediation of a priest. After Adam's fall (see Gen. 3), the way to God was barred. Access through this barrier is possible only through God's Son, Jesus Christ (see John 14:6).

The Levitical priesthood of the Old Testament was merely a picture of Jesus' high priestly function. Moses revealed that the imperfect, mortal high priest could only enter the Holy of Holies once a year on what is today called Yom Kippur (see Lev. 16). Because the perfect High Priest, Jesus Christ, has replaced that picture, we can now enter the Holy of Holies through Him.

Figure 9

The Comparison of the Priesthood of Christ with that of Aaron		
Qualifications	**Aaron**	**Christ**
1. Selected from men (5:1)	Tribe of Levi	Incarnate
2. Offers for sins (5:1)	Many sacrifices (5:1)	Perfect Sacrifice (5:9)
3. Deals gently with sinners (5:2)	Was a sinner (5:3)	Able to save (5:9)
4. God appointed (5:4)	Those in Aaron's line (5:4)	After the order of Melchizedek (5:10)

Figure 9 compares the priesthood of Jesus Christ with that of Aaron. We see in it four distinct features.

1. Every high priest had to be chosen from among men. Man sinned, and man had to pay the penalty of sin. "It is impossible for the blood of bulls and of goats to take away sins" (Heb. 10:4). Each man can pay the penalty for his own sin, but at the price of spending an eternity separated from God. So the high priest after the order of Aaron, from the tribe of Levi, was inadequate, since he too was a sinner and couldn't even atone for his own sin. This in itself points to the necessity for Christ, His incarnation, and His atoning ministry.

2. The high priest's function was to offer sacrifices to God for sin. In this capacity, the Levitical priesthood was ineffective in that it could only offer animals as token sacrifices. This resulted in their sacrificing day after day without any hope of their efforts ever obtaining the forgiveness sought after. Jesus, however, is not only our High Priest but is also our Perfect Sacrifice. He was able to offer "for all time one sacrifice for sins" (Heb. 10:12).

3. Both Aaron and Christ met the qualification of dealing gently with the ignorant. The difficulty with Aaron's priesthood lay in the fact that he was part of the problem rather than part of the solution. He could deal gently with sinners, but he also needed gentleness shown to him.

4. No man took on himself the honor of serving as high priest. God chose His own high priest. Just as God chose Aaron from the tribe of Levi, so He chose Christ. In choosing Him, however, God did not select from a human tribe with all its limitations; instead, Jesus was "in the order of Melchizedek." He had a perfect high priestly lineage.

In summary, though both Aaron and Jesus Christ met the qualifications for the office of high priest, they differed in the way they were able to function. Christ was a perfect High Priest because He could offer a perfect sacrifice. Aaron was limited in that his sacrifice could never solve man's problem of sin. This difference in the kind of sacrifice Jesus could offer is the subject of the next paragraph.

Qualifications of the Perfect Sacrifice — *Hebrews 5:5-10*

[5]So Christ also did not take upon himself the glory of becoming a high priest. But God said to him,

"You are my Son;

Today I have become your Father."

[6]And he says in another place,

"You are a priest forever,
in the order of Melchizedek."

[7]During the days of Jesus' life on earth, he offered up prayers and petitions with loud cries and tears to the one who could save him from death, and he was heard because of his reverent submission. [8]Although he was a son, he learned obedience from what he suffered, [9]and once made perfect, he became the source of eternal salvation for all who obey him [10]and was designated by God to be high priest, just like Melchizedek.

The theme of this paragraph pivots about verse seven. Certain events occurred when our Lord was on earth; His offering up "prayers and petitions with loud cries and tears" takes us back to those traumatic moments in Gethsemane the night when He was betrayed. There in the garden our Savior prayed, "My Father, if it is possible, may this cup be taken from me" (Matt. 26:39). On His knees before the Father, He experienced the anguish of the coming death, mounting to such a point that He sweat, as it were, drops of blood.

Why? What made the prospect of death such a trauma? If His was solely the death of a martyr, then Jesus' attitude in facing the cross was far less noble than that of many men and women who have walked the narrow road to martyrdom. Many have faced a similar fate without pleading with God for a way of escape.

To understand the issue facing Jesus that night in Gethsemane, we need to realize that two kinds of death face us—spiritual and physical. Physical death takes place when the soul is separated from the body. If you were to look at the body of a dead person, perhaps someone you knew well, he would appear exactly as you had seen him many times before. The hair is combed in the same way, the clothes are familiar, his face appears no different; he seems to be the same person you knew. Yet, though the body is there, the real person has departed. In physical death, the soul, or the "real person," is separated from the body.

Likewise, spiritual death takes place when the soul is separated from God. Sin's major accompanying characteristic is that it separates; it always has and it always will. For example, in a husband-wife relationship if one partner is promiscuous, the result may be a divorce, because a separation has taken place. In the spiritual realm, unregenerate man is separated from God because of his sin. We refer to him as being dead spiritually (see Eph. 2:1). It is possible for a person to be alive physically but dead spiritually.

Because both physical and spiritual death are the fruits of sin, it was necessary for Jesus, in His substitutionary death for man, to die both physically and spiritually. When Jesus went to the cross, He experienced death in both realms.

The trauma, however, that Jesus experienced in the Garden of Gethsemane was not the prospect of physical death. Had He not already raised Lazarus and others from the dead? Having demonstrated His ability to conquer physical death, how could it be fear of going through it Himself that caused drops of blood to pour down His face?

No, it was the prospect of spiritual death that caused Him such agony. To say that Jesus experienced such a death is to suggest that the Godhead was rent in two—God the Son was separated from God the Father. Hanging on that Roman gibbet, Jesus cried, "My God, my God, why have you forsaken me?" (Matt. 27:46)

On His knees, beneath the twisted trunks and branches of the olive trees in that lovely garden, Jesus pondered the implications of such a separation—a broken relationship in the Godhead; never in all eternity had such a thing happened. "Father, is it possible for this cup to pass from Me? Is there some way that We can accomplish Our objective without paying such a high price?"

It was not a martyr's death Jesus was to experience on the cross. He was to take a risk that would dwarf the faith of the greatest men of God who had gone before Him. Once separated from God, would it be possible to be reunited? What agony! The God-man, perfect in all His ways, unworthy of such a sentence, judged guilty. "God made him who had no sin to be sin for us, so that in him we might become the righteousness of God" (2 Cor. 5:21).

As we trace the sequence of events on that Good Friday, we notice that Christ died spiritually *before* dying physically. The former took place on the cross when He cried, "My God, my God, why have you forsaken me?" Spiritual death took place because God broke the relationship with His Son, who had been made sin on our behalf.

Next we observe that Jesus Christ was resurrected spiritually *before* He died physically. While Jesus was talking to the two thieves hanging next to Him, one requested, "Jesus, remember me when you come into your kingdom." Jesus said to him, "I tell you the truth, today you will be with me in paradise'' (Luke 23:42,43). Notice that Jesus said ''today'' not ''in three days' time,'' when He was resurrected physically on Easter morning. The man entered paradise with Jesus on Good Friday.

Jesus was able to make this promise because minutes later He pronounced, ''It is finished!'' (John 19:30) What was finished? The work of redemption. In taking our sins on Himself, Jesus satisfied God's wrath against sin. Having *finished* the work of our redemption, Jesus cried, '' 'Father, into your hands I commit my spirit.' When he had said this, he breathed his last'' (Luke 23:46).

When Jesus died physically, Matthew records a strange event: ''At that moment the curtain of the temple was torn in two from top to bottom'' (Matt. 27:51). That it was torn from top to bottom and not vice versa is important, for it signifies that it was God, not man, who tore the veil. This took place on Friday afternoon immediately after Jesus' death, not on Sunday morning when the stone was rolled away from the tomb.

The Holy Spirit was communicating that at the very moment the veil separating the Holy of Holies from the sanctuary was torn in two, all believers everywhere obtained access into the immediate presence of God. Jesus' sacrifice had been accepted; God's justice was satisfied; redemption was complete; the sinner was reconciled to his God.

Christ having accomplished redemption through His agonizing spiritual separation from the Father, the broken relationship was restored. ''Into your hands I commit my spirit'' was the way He put it. Surrendering to physical death then became easy, for Satan was defeated, our salvation was assured, and Jesus had already been resurrected spiritually.

If Jesus' work of redemption was accomplished on Friday, what then was the significance of Easter Sunday? The physical resurrection of our Lord is for our benefit. Here is God's guarantee that what Jesus said while hanging on the cross actually happened. If He had not been resurrected physically, we would never know certainly if what He promised actually took place.

The physical resurrection attests to the reality of the spiritual resurrection. For had Jesus not been resurrected spiritually, had Satan rather than Christ won the contest on Golgotha, Jesus could not have resurrected Himself physically any more than you can resurrect yourself physically once you have died.

We celebrate Easter because it is our guarantee that all is well between the sinner and God.

Returning again to the key verse of this paragraph, we read, "During the days of Jesus' life on earth, he offered up prayers and petitions with loud cries and tears to the one who could save him from death, and he was heard because of his reverent submission" (Heb. 5:7). His submission was an attitude of awe and reverence. Our Lord respected the will of God for His life and followed through with it even at the dreadful price of the cross. It was at Gethsemane, the night before the cross, that Jesus wrestled with the issues and settled on the only course of action that could insure our salvation.

"Although he was a son, he learned obedience" (v. 8). The ultimate test of faith is obedience. Faith is the action of obeying what you know to be the will of God. It is interesting that the author used the word *learned*. Obedience is an attitude that must be learned. It has to be taught to us. As a man, Jesus had to learn just as we do.

Luke affords us an insight into this truth when he wrote, "And Jesus grew in wisdom and stature, and in favor with God and men" (Luke 2:52). These were the four areas in which the man Jesus learned: wisdom (intellectual), stature (physical), favor with man (social), and favor with God (spiritual). He wasn't born completely developed in these areas. For Him, life was a learning process in the school of obedience.

Jesus' example of obedience on the cross shows us to what extent we should submit to God and obey Him.

Then we are told the result of Jesus' obedient faith: "And once made perfect, he became the source of eternal salvation for all who obey him" (Heb. 5:9). His perfection qualified Him to be the source of our salvation. Perfection was the very thing that the Old Testament high priest could never attain. Because Jesus is perfect, He didn't have to die for His own sins and could, therefore, offer Himself as a sacrifice for the sins of the people. Because Jesus is God, His sacrifice is sufficient to pay for the sins of all mankind—past, present, and future. The perfect High Priest offered the perfect sacrifice and in so doing became the source of our salvation.

Referring to Figure 8 on page 60, we see in verses 1-4 the *requirements*, and in verses 5-10 the *requirements met*. In the first section we reviewed the *temporal* priesthood; in the second, the *eternal* priesthood. Because of their imperfection, Old Testament priests *offered animals;* but Jesus, being perfect, *offered Himself*. In verses 1-4, the emphasis is on *Aaron,* and in verses 5-10, on *Christ.* In the third and final section we will see that the emphasis is on the *believer.*

Qualifications for Maturity — *Hebrews 5:11-14*

> [11]We have much to say about this, but it is hard to explain because you are slow to learn. [12]In fact, though by this time you ought to be teachers, you need someone to teach you the elementary truths of God's word all over again. You need milk, not solid food! [13]Anyone who lives on milk, being still an infant, is not acquainted with the teaching about righteousness. [14]But solid food is for the mature, who by constant use have trained themselves to distinguish good from evil.

In this section, which is the third warning in the book—Maturity Affects Assurance—the writer laments that he is faced with two problems among his readers. The first is stated like this: "We have much to say about this, but it is hard to explain" (v. 11). In the previous passages, we have been probing some deep truths—truths in the category of "solid food," not "milk." Understanding them requires some chewing. But the writer seems to be suggesting that he has only been able to feed us with "milk" (vv. 12-13). If this is "milk" and we are finding it like "solid food," it reveals how shallow we are in our comprehension of the Word.

As we seek to grow in our understanding of the Scriptures, it is easy to compare ourselves with fellow believers. Such a comparison is subjective and valueless (see 2 Cor. 10:12). The Holy Spirit wants us to evaluate ourselves with a more objective standard, and in this passage we have one: our ability to comprehend what the writer is saying. Such a challenge should motivate us to a far deeper commitment to the Word of God.

The second problem is stated thus: "Because you are slow to learn" (v. 11). Dullness is the result of sloth. It is a testimony to the fact that we don't listen attentively to what God has to say. The writer is talking to Christians who refuse to grow up spiritually. Content to drink milk all their lives, they never learn how to chew solid food. Feeding a baby with a bottle of milk is fun, but it becomes tragic when that "baby" is twenty years old.

Some of you may have been walking with Jesus ten, fifteen, or possibly twenty years, yet are still drinking spiritual milk. The only knowledge you have of the Bible is what you have been taught by others. You have never learned to feed yourself from the Word of

God. To the degree that this is true of you, let this picture used by the writer stir you to action.

Maturity and growth are expressions of the will. Most people can grow if they are willing to pay the price. For those who long for maturity and growth in their spiritual lives, the writer has two suggestions:

1. "Leave the elementary teachings about Christ and go on to maturity" (Heb. 6:1). Become deeply committed to being in the Word of God. Sink the roots of your soul into the Scriptures. This is a sure road to maturity.

2. "Who by constant use . . ." (Heb. 5:14). Apply what you learn. Just as a coin has a "head" and "tail" on it, so also is the "coin" of maturity. One side is "depth in the Word"; the other is "applying what the Word teaches." The ability "to distinguish good from evil" is granted to the person who has studied the issues and developed the habit of doing what is right no matter what the price may be.

Where do you stand in your maturity in the Word as you evaluate yourself by God's standard in Hebrews 5? If the Holy Spirit is speaking to you on this issue, follow the example of Jesus and *obey* Him.

HEBREWS 5:11–6:20

Figure 10

THE PROMISES OF CHRIST
(His Is a Better Assurance)
Hebrews 5:11 — 6:20

Basis of Works — Basis of Salvation

WARNING: MATURITY AFFECTS ASSURANCE			MATURITY BELIEVES GOD'S WORD
FAILURE TO MATURE	FINDING ASSURANCE	FEELINGS OF ASSURANCE	FOUNDATION OF ASSURANCE
5:11-14	6:1-6	6:7-12	6:13-20
Exhortation		Encouragement	
Hindrances		Hope	
Works for Salvation		Works After Salvation	Work of Salvation
Immaturity		Imitating	Immutability
Importance of Maturity	Importance of Understanding	Importance of Good Works	Importance of God's Promise

5

THE PROMISES OF CHRIST

As we progress through Hebrews, we come to the often-troublesome chapter 6. Some people tend to treat it as if it were a mysterious, dark tunnel and shy away from attempting to interpret its meaning; others who probe its depths often come away thinking the chapter teaches that a person can lose his salvation.

If we are to come to grips with the issues in this passage, particularly in verses 4-6, we must first attempt to understand the context in which the chapter is set. Figure 11 on page 74 should help us.

The horizontal line in the middle of the page separating "belief" from "unbelief" crystallizes the key issue in chapters 3 and 4. In summary, belief resulted in unbroken fellowship with God on a day-by-day basis, unbelief in wandering in the wilderness of broken fellowship. The first response brings the believer into God's rest; the latter bars him entrance.

In chapter 3, we met Israel at Kadesh Barnea at the very threshold of the Promised Land. An encounter with the giants made the Israelites lose heart and doubt God's promise. This expression of unbelief broke fellowship with God and resulted in the tragic forty-year wandering in the wilderness. Outside the Promised Land, unable to reclaim God's promise, with an unclear position, and a lack of assurance, the Hebrew nation wandered aimlessly around till every person guilty of unbelief had died.

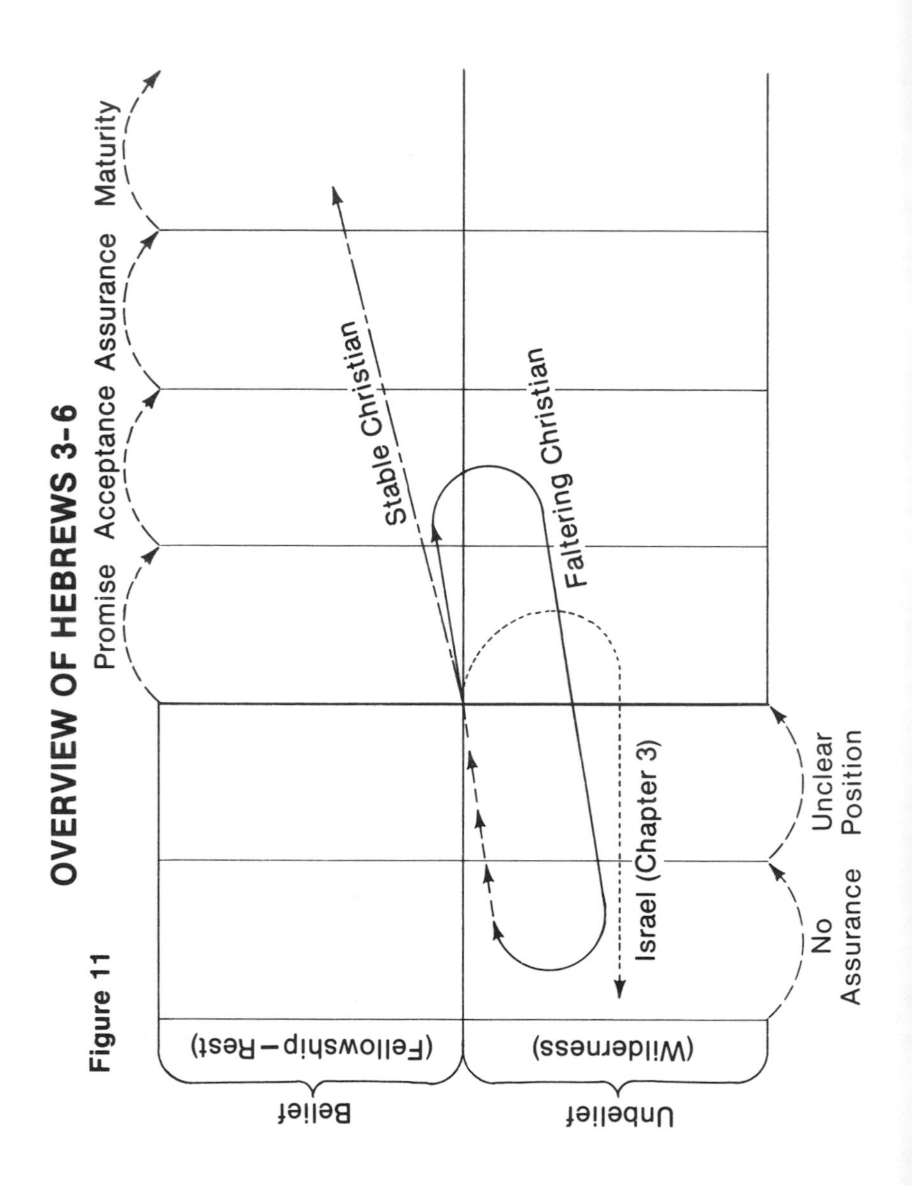

Figure 11

OVERVIEW OF HEBREWS 3-6

What happened to Israel can happen to any believer today. This was the theme of chapter 4. God's rest has been made available to every generation—a rest entered by believing God's promises. (We will do well to remind ourselves that *fellowship* and not *salvation* is the point in question. Not all those buried in the wilderness lost their salvation—for example, Moses, Aaron, Miriam. What they missed out on was the blessing of God on their lives.)

After emphasizing the timelessness of God's rest, the writer in chapter 4 went on to discuss one of the most common obstacles the Christian faces in entering that rest, namely, the realization that he is totally and unconditionally accepted by God. Jesus Christ accepts us for who we are—not for who He wants us to be. Acceptance in the presence of our Lord is not on the basis of what we do for Him but on what He has done and is continuing to do for us.

I know myself better than anyone else does. This makes accepting myself extremely hard. In fact, it is so hard that I can only do so by faith, by believing that when God says He loves and accepts me, He really means it.

I know what sort of man I am—sinful, vulgar, vile, and fully capable of committing every sin listed in the Bible. I am my own worst enemy. I make myself sick! So when God counters my feelings with "I know the way you are, but nevertheless I accept you," He blows every circuit in my computer.

If I allow this great truth to slip out of my hands by doubting God's veracity, I revert to unbelief and follow Israel into a wilderness experience. Hence the writer's admonition, "Therefore, since the promise of entering his rest still stands, let us be careful that none of you be found to have fallen short of it" (Heb. 4:1). Figure 11 on page 74 portrays it. To ignore this admonition is to become a "faltering Christian."

Jesus Christ makes possible my acceptance by God. This is His function as my High Priest. The writer of Hebrews keeps reviewing this high priestly work of our Lord. In chapter 2, the writer informed us that it was Jesus who destroyed the works of the devil (v. 14), delivered us from bondage (v. 15), reconciled us to God (v. 17), and in so doing graced us with unhindered access into His presence.

Chapters 3–10 portray various facets of this great truth. It is the stable Christian (Figure 11, page 74) who has grasped its implications and has, therefore, moved on from assurance to maturity.

Chapter 5, however, closes with the writer expressing his frustration over his readers' immaturity. After referring to Figure 10 on page 72, let us pick up his argument with which he opens his third warning (Heb. 5:11).

Failure to Mature — *Hebrews 5:11-14*

> [11]We have much to say about this, but it is hard to explain because you are slow to learn. [12]In fact, though by this time you ought to be teachers, you need someone to teach you the elementary truths of God's word all over again. You need milk, not solid food! [13]Anyone who lives on milk, being still an infant, is not acquainted with the teaching about righteousness. [14]But solid food is for the mature, who by constant use have trained themselves to distinguish good from evil.

The writer is obviously not referring to stable, growing Christians. Chronologically, those described are old enough to be teachers, but spiritually they are still on pabulum and warm milk. He pinpoints the problem in the phrase "by constant *use*" (v. 14). The writer's recipients were that way because they had failed to apply the Word of God to their lives. The process of studying the Word and applying it is precisely what is needed to insure healthy development and maturity. Maturity in turn yields the understanding necessary to study and apply still more of the Word. There is a spiral effect here—the more you learn and apply, the more you find you are able to learn and apply.

Yet the ones addressed in this section have been derailed from this maturing spiral.

Finding Assurance — *Hebrews 6:1-6*

> [1]Therefore let us leave the elementary teachings about Christ and go on to maturity. Let us not lay again the foundation of repentance from acts that lead to death, and of faith in God, [2]instruction about baptisms, the laying on of hands, the resurrection of the dead, and eternal judgment. [3]And God permitting, we will do so.
>
> [4]It is impossible for those who have once been enlightened, who have tasted the heavenly gift, who have shared in the Holy Spirit, [5]who have tasted the goodness of the word of God and the powers of the coming age, [6]if they fall away, to be brought back to repentance, [seeing that] they are crucifying the Son of God all over again and subjecting him to public disgrace.

The opening clause gives us a clue as to what is wrong. The people in question were laying "again the foundation of repentance from acts that lead to death, and of faith in God'' (v. 1). A person ''repents from acts that lead to death'' when in desperation he admits his spiritual bankruptcy and declares that he has placed his total faith in God. This constitutes the believer's conversion experience. God makes a *promise:* ''Everyone who calls on the name of the Lord will be saved'' (Rom. 10:13). The seeker *believes* that promise (or one similar to it), and calls on the name of the Lord, and is thereby saved.

Once saved, the believer now finds himself on the long road toward Christian maturity. Filled with assurance, he begins to study and apply the Scriptures. But after a while he finds that things are not going quite the way he had hoped they would. Possibly his frustration stems from a nagging sin he seems unable to overcome, or from a cloud of doubt cast by another who believes that science refutes the authority of the Bible, or from any one of a dozen other things. But whatever the cause, the result is always the same—*guilt.* Guilt in turn leads to introspection. The faltering Christian finds himself thinking ''If I were *really* a Christian, I wouldn't have done this. Maybe I wasn't ever really saved.'' Instead of believing God's unchanging promises, he chooses to acknowledge the feelings generated by his bad experiences. He begins to waver and then capitulates into a wilderness of unbelief (see Figure 11, page 74).

Whatever the surface reasons, the root problem is always the same: ''Can God *really* accept me when I am so sinful?'' Yes, of course He can, and He does. ''My acceptance of you is based on what Jesus Christ did, not on what you do'' is God's rebuttal to your doubt.

A failure to grasp this results in the Christian returning to the cross in a desperate search for another conversion experience, or as the writer says, ''Laying *again* the foundation of repentance from dead works and of faith toward God'' (KJV). Figure 11 illustrates this pattern.

The faltering Christian goes around and around in circles as he repeatedly cuts himself off from maturity when he comes to the stumbling block of self-acceptance and so reverts to a position of no assurance. Months and years go by, but no forward motion is achieved.

Every building must have a foundation, but only *one* foundation is needed. Lay it once and lay it well. Having laid the foundation, don't periodically try to relay it. Get on with building the structure. The foundation of your Christian life will hold; it was built on the very promise of God and not on your own personal experience. ''Therefore,'' says the writer, ''let us . . . go on to maturity'' (Heb. 6:1).

How then do I, as a believer, find assurance? By trusting in the objective truth of God's promises rather than relying on the subjective feelings that come from my own experiences. When guilt and doubt begin to erode my assurance, I should quench my feelings and instead take counsel from God's Word.

Note the parallels between *doctrines* (vv. 1-2) and *experiences* (vv. 4-5) in this passage (Figure 12).

Figure 12

Doctrine	Experiences
Repentance, faith	Been enlightened
Baptism	Tasted the heavenly gift
Laying on of hands	Shared in the Holy Spirit
Resurrection of the dead	Tasted the Word of God
Eternal judgment	Tasted the powers of the coming age

If you have experienced the doctrines that are foundational in that they deal with becoming a Christian, then you have been saved. Combining verse 4 with verse 6, we read: ''It is impossible for those who [have experienced salvation] if they fall away, to be brought back to repentance.''

The Greek word for *fall away* (v. 6) has the same meaning as the word used for *depart* in Hebrews 3:12, namely, ''to offend,'' ''to fall,'' ''to sin.'' In short, the idea in chapter 6 is the same as in chapter 3. It refers to the child of God who has failed to believe God's promises and obey His commands.

Of such people the writer says, ''It is impossible . . . [for them] to be brought back to repentance.'' The word *repentance* is the same as that used in verse 1. It conveys the idea of moving first in one direction and then in another; it is synonymous with conversion.

In summary, the writer is saying that when a Christian falls into sin, it is impossible for him to be renewed through another conversion experience, because that would be equivalent to ''crucifying the Son of God all over again and subjecting him to public disgrace'' (v. 6).

To help bring this into focus, let me pose a question. When you became a Christian, where did you go for your conversion experience? I am speaking theologically, not geographically. You answer correctly, ''To the cross of Christ.'' As one hymnwriter puts it, ''Nothing in my hands I bring; simply to Thy cross I cling.''

As a Christian, you sin. The process of sanctification will gradually deliver you from the power of sin, but never from the presence of sin. In one of his last letters, Paul called himself the worst of sinners (see 1 Tim. 1:15). Where do you go for forgiveness? The writer answers this question: ''Let us therefore come boldly unto the throne of grace, that we may obtain mercy, and find grace to help in time of need'' (Heb. 4:16).

As Christians, we don't return to the cross for a fresh conversion experience every time we sin, as this would be tantamount to crucifying ''the Son of God afresh and putting Him to an open shame'' (v. 6 KJV). Rather, as believers who have sinned, we go to ''the throne of grace with confidence, so that we may receive mercy and find grace to help us in our time of need'' (Heb. 4:16).

This is a great source of encouragement and assurance. Fellowship broken by sin and unbelief doesn't carry with it the loss of salvation. When we backslide and grieve God, forgiveness is guaranteed simply by our coming to the throne of grace.

In review, it is impossible for you as a Christian seeking forgiveness to come to the cross for another conversion experience. This would be like repeatedly crucifying Jesus Christ, making a mockery of His atoning death.

The application is obvious. Filled with assurance, as a stable Christian, press on toward maturity. Stop being preoccupied with the ABCs of the Christian life. The cross is empty. Don't try to hang Jesus on it again. His atoning sacrifice is sufficient to handle *all* your sins—past, present, and future.

Feelings of Assurance — *Hebrews 6:7-12*

[7]Land that drinks in the rain often falling on it and that produces a crop useful to those who farm it receives the blessing of God. [8]But land that produces thorns and thistles is worthless and is [near to] being cursed. In the end it will be burned.

[9]Even though we speak like this, dear friends, we are confident of better things in your case—things that accompany salvation. [10]God is not unjust; he will not forget your work and the

> love you have shown him as you have helped his people and continue to help them. [11]We want each of you to show this same diligence to the very end, in order to make your hope sure. [12]We do not want you to become lazy, but to imitate those who through faith and patience inherit what has been promised.

Though our assurance is based on fact and not on our feelings, there is an important place for feelings in the Christian life. This is the next point with which the writer deals.

The assurance that I feel in my relationship with God is not just dependent on proper doctrine. Proper works also play an important role. In any interpersonal exchange, how I behave myself with the other person has a definite effect on our relationship. This is where *works* come into the Christian life.

In verse 1, we are exhorted to repent "from acts that lead to death." These are the works of self-effort that seek to build a ladder to heaven. Any attempt I make to merit salvation by my own efforts is a repudiation of Christ's perfect work. They are acts that lead to death and are to be repented of.

Having discussed the basis of our relationship with God (v. 1-6), the writer says that *following* salvation, works play an important part. To use an old proverb, the cart (works) must follow the horse (salvation). If you reverse these two, you will destroy your assurance and hinder your maturity.

To bring this point home, the writer paints a picture for us (vv. 7-8). In the analogy, the Christian is represented by the earth. The fruit of the earth (herbs, thorns, briers) are the *works* of the Christian. God's response to our works is either blessing or burning.

If the believer's life produces good works (herbs), God will reward him. If, however, the Christian produces bad works (thorns and briers), God will reject them; they will be cursed (note that *he* is not cursed but comes very close) and "in the end [they] will be burned" (v. 8).

In a forest fire the earth itself is not burned, just the "fruit of the earth." This is the point of the analogy. If you produce things in your life that are not acceptable to God, those fruits will be burned. The Christian life that produces godly works will be accepted by the Lord and these works will remain. Paul communicated the same truth to the Corinthians:

> For no one can lay any foundation other than the one already laid, which is Jesus Christ. If any man builds on this foundation using gold, silver, costly stones, wood, hay or straw, his work will be shown for

> what it is, because the Day will bring it to light. It will be revealed by fire, and the fire will test the quality of each man's work. If what he has built survives, he will receive his reward. If it is burned up, he will suffer loss; he himself will be saved, but only as one escaping through the flames (1 Cor. 3:11-15).

If the Christian's work is "wood, hay or straw," it will be burned. But notice, "He himself will be *saved,* but only as one escaping through the flames." Our works have nothing to do with our salvation, but they determine the quality of life we live.

The fact of assurance is a by-product of Jesus' finished work on the cross. Our feelings of assurance are by-products of good works. Good works do not contribute to the *fact;* they simply enhance the *feelings.*

Having established the place of works in the Christian life, that they are "things that *accompany* salvation" (Heb. 6:9), the writer goes on to encourage those good works, "God . . . will not forget your works" (v. 10). So you should "show this same diligence," for they "make your hope sure" (v. 11).

Every Christian should be a follower; we are to emulate the works of those who have become heirs to God's promises (v. 12). What are we to imitate? Their *faith* and *patience.* Whose faith and patience are you imitating? Is your faith and patience of such a quality that the Holy Spirit can encourage others to follow you?

Foundation of Assurance — *Hebrews 6:13-20*

> [13]When God made his promise to Abraham, since there was no one greater for him to swear by, he swore by himself, [14]saying, "I will surely bless you and give you many descendants." [15]And so after waiting patiently, Abraham received what was promised.
>
> [16]Men swear by someone greater than themselves, and the oath confirms what is said and puts an end to all argument. [17]Because God wanted to make the unchanging nature of his purpose very clear to the heirs of what was promised, he confirmed it with an oath. [18]God did this so that, by two unchangeable things in which it is impossible for God to lie, we who have fled to take hold of the hope offered to us may be greatly encouraged. [19]We have this hope as an anchor for the soul, firm and secure. It enters the inner sanctuary behind the curtain, [20]where Jesus, who went before us, has entered on our behalf. He has become a high priest forever, in the order of Melchizedek.

In biblical times, before the day of attorneys, title companies, and other modern institutions, people settled their disagreements by coming to a mutual understanding and then confirming it with a promise. Such an oath or promise was final in its authority and, says the writer, brought an end to all strife (v. 16 KJV).

God followed this procedure one day when He appeared to Abraham with a promise. To assure Abraham that He meant what He said, He sealed His promise with an oath. The Lord couldn't swear by a mountain saying, "As long as this mountain stands, you will know that My promise to you is unchanging," for He knew that one day the mountain would be no more. The same was true for the sky, trees, the whole planet, and all other created things. So, "since there was no one greater for him to swear by, he swore by himself" (v. 13). "The fact that I said it," declared God, "is the greatest guarantee I can give you." God's promises are absolutely reliable.

One of the most precious possessions a man has is his good name (Prov. 22:1). To perjure himself or refuse to fulfill a promise should be unthinkable. The guarantee of our salvation is based on the assurance that God will never do such a thing to us.

Two unchanging things make it impossible for God to lie. These two immutable things are His *counsel* and His *oath*.

Through the predetermined foreknowledge of God, His work was completed before the foundation of the world (Heb. 4:3). History is simply the unfolding of His divine plan (counsel), which is unchanging (Heb. 6:17).

Not only did our sovereign Lord plan all things in His counsel from the foundation of the world, He also "confirmed it with an oath" (v. 17). Long before Abraham's birth, God had decided to bless him and make him the father of the Hebrew nation. Later, He personally confirmed this plan to Abraham with an oath when He said, "I will surely bless you and give you many descendants" (v. 14).

"By two unchangeable things [His counsel and oath] in which it is impossible for God to lie, we . . . may be greatly encouraged" (v. 18). God decreed it; God promised it; and it happened.

Referring back now to Figure 10 on page 72, we see that the second and fourth sections (vv. 1-6, 13-20) reveal the *basis of salvation;* this is the substitutionary death of Christ on the cross, decreed eternally by God from the foundation of the world and promised again and again in the Scriptures.

The first and third sections (Heb. 5:11-14, 6:7-12) emphasize the *basis of works*. Good works in the Christian life are a great help in the maturing process and at the same time contribute to our feelings of assurance.

In the first part of the section, we hear God's *exhortation;* in the second, His *encouragement*. In the first, we see two major hindrances to assurance: immaturity and unbelief; in the second, we note the *hope* we have as an anchor of the soul.

Then reflect on Hebrews 5:11–6:6 and note how *works for salvation* will hamper our maturity as well as destroy our assurance. *Works after salvation* are important, however, and are discussed in Hebrews 6:7-12. The *work of salvation* (Heb. 6:13-20) belongs to God and to Him alone. In each of the four parts, an *important* truth is driven home: *maturity, understanding, good works,* and *God's promise*. These four combine to provide a better assurance.

As we bring this chapter to a close, meditate with me on one of the most beautiful truths in Hebrews (see Heb. 6:19-20). The picture is that of an ancient sailing vessel finding its way through the narrow entrance to a harbor. This was one of the trickiest maneuvers the captain of a ship had to make. As his ship moved through the opening, he had to guard against a gust of wind running it onto a reef or a sandbar. The skeleton of many a ship could be seen on the rocks, giving testimony to the fact that its captain had failed his navigation test.

To minimize the risk, the olden-day skipper would lower the ship's anchor into a smaller boat, which would then be rowed through the narrow entrance of the harbor. The anchor would then be dropped and the ship, with sails down, would be pulled past the obstacles, through the narrow opening, and into the safety of the harbor.

What Jesus Christ, as your High Priest, has done is analogous to this maritime illustration. The Savior as your Anchor, "both sure and stedfast," has already entered the harbor "into that within the veil," the Holy of Holies, the very presence of God. As your Anchor, He will never be moved. He has ahold of you and is pulling you into His presence on a day-by-day basis. Storms and anxious moments will come, but your assurance is based on the fact that your life is tied to His. With a watchful eye, He guarantees your safe arrival into the harbor of His presence. You don't have to worry about being shipwrecked on the rocks of unbelief or the sandbars of sin. You can be absolutely sure that no matter how turbulent the situation, the Anchor of your soul will hold.

Remember, your assurance is not based on your ability to effect holiness in your own life. Rather, it is founded on the promise that the total process for your redemption is in the capable hands of God.

HEBREWS 7:1–28

THE PERFECTION OF CHRIST
(His Is a Better Priesthood)
Hebrews 7

Figure 13

HIS PERSON		HIS PROMISE		HIS PERFORMANCE	
Credentials of Melchizedek	Consideration of His Greatness	Change Needed in the Old Order	Covenant Established by an Oath	Contrasting Abilities in the Priesthoods	Christ's Sacrifice of Himself
7:1-3	7:4-10	7:11-19	7:20-22	7:23-25	7:26-28
Better Order		Better Covenant		Better Priest	
Who He Was		Why He Came		What He Did	
Because He Is From Melchizedek		He Is Not Limited by Sinai		He Is Not Limited by the Altar	

6

THE PERFECTION OF CHRIST

Abraham and Lot, because of a quarrel between their herdsmen, had separated. But the kings of Mesopotamia should have known better than to try to take advantage of that. In their wars of plunder, these eastern kings had pillaged the little communities that had sprung up along the fertile shores of the Jordan River. After his separation from his uncle Abraham, Lot and his family settled in one of these towns and fell victim to the raiding kings from the east. They were taken prisoner and were on their way to a life of exile and slavery.

One of the servants who had escaped made his way to the tent of Abraham with the sad news, and "When Abram heard that his relative had been taken captive, he called out the 318 trained men born in his household and went in pursuit as far as Dan" (Gen. 14:14).

Coming upon the plundering parties, drunk with success, Abraham and his small party attacked late at night. The results were predictable. Those of the enemy who were not slaughtered fled for their lives. Lot and all of his family were rescued.

Excitement and thanksgiving swelled the hearts of that successful family as they made their way home. Then suddenly, out of nowhere, a stranger appeared, bearing with him bread and wine. His name was Melchizedek. "He was priest of God Most High, and he blessed Abram saying, 'Blessed be Abram by God Most High, Creator of heaven and earth. And blessed be God Most High, who delivered your enemies into your hand.' " (Gen. 14:18-20).

A strange thing followed. For no apparent reason and without any prompting, Abraham gave Melchizedek "tithes of all." Then as mysteriously as he came, he disappeared. There is no record of Abraham having ever met him before or again. Nothing else is said of him in the Old Testament except for a messianic statement about Christ, "The Lord has sworn and will not change his mind: 'You are a priest forever, in the order of Melchizedek' " (Ps. 110:4).

Who was this mysterious figure Melchizedek? Why did he appear to Abraham? What happened to him after that encounter? Why is he mentioned in Psalm 110:4? Why does the writer assume that we know more about Melchizedek than we do when he introduced him earlier (see Heb. 5:6)? These tantalizing questions are answered for us by the Holy Spirit in this passage (Heb. 7).

The recurring theme that emerges from this section is that Jesus Christ's priesthood is perfect because it has its origin in the priesthood of Melchizedek. Using Figure 13 on page 86, we see that his perfect priesthood can be looked at in His Person (vv. 1-10), His Promise (vv. 11-22), and His Performance (vv. 23-28).

His Person

The first part centers on Melchizedek's person and origin (vv. 1-10). No mention is made of Jesus Christ till later (vv. 11-28), where it is emphasized that His priesthood is better than the Levitical priesthood because it has its origin in Melchizedek. The tie-in is based entirely on the messianic reference in Psalm 110:4.

Credentials of Melchizedek — Hebrews 7:1-3

> [1]This Melchizedek was king of Salem and a priest of God Most High. He met Abraham returning from the defeat of the kings and blessed him, [2]and Abraham gave him a tenth of everything. First, his name means "king of righteousness"; then also, "king of Salem" means "king of peace." [3]Without father or mother, without beginning of days or end of life, like the Son of God he remains a priest forever.

These verses provide a commentary on Abraham's encounter with Melchizedek in Genesis 14. Some of what is said here can easily be drawn from the Genesis narrative; the rest is additional insight provided by the writer to the Hebrews through the illumination of the Holy Spirit.

Melchizedek blessed Abraham (v. 1.) It is interesting that the father of the Hebrews through whom Christ descended, the recipient of an unconditional divine covenant of grace, the "friend of God," should be blessed by Melchizedek. You would think it should have been the other way around in the light of the Old Testament custom of the greater blessing the lesser.

Melchizedek is not only a priest but a king (v. 2). He is "King of righteousness, King of Salem, King of Peace." *Salem* is the ancient name for the holy city Jerusalem. As king of this city, he is also king of "righteousness" and "peace." Not *was*, but *is*, for the writer suggests that his is an eternal priesthood (v. 3).

This comment on peace and righteousness is indeed a remarkable declaration in view of our current world situation. Our generation is characterized by its search for the elusive "Alchemist's Stone," which could turn strife instantly to peace. We are surrounded on all sides by would-be experts in the art of seeking and making peace.

Many advocate *escape,* in every form imaginable. Television, movies, sports events, and travel are just a few ways of "getting away from it all." The problem with the "escape" technique is that reality always awaits your return.

Evasion is another well-tried technique in achieving peace. "Refuse to think about it," we are told. But what really happens is that everything gets bottled up inside us. It's like trying to put too much air in a tire—you run the risk of a blow-out. As the pressure mounts, you become a candidate for an emotional breakdown or worse.

Diplomacy and *compromise* are advocated as techniques to use on both interpersonal and international levels. "Give a little—take a little" is the philosophy of this approach. Too often it proves to be the catalyst that destroys rather than creates peace. The United States' involvement in Vietnam was a clear illustration of this.

God's solution to the lack of peace is always the same—*righteousness*. Righteousness and peace are the two sides of the same coin in the divine economy. "The fruit of righteousness will be peace; the effect of righteousness will be quietness and confidence forever. My people will live in peaceful dwelling places" (Isa. 32:17-18). Righteousness removes the problem of why there is no peace.

The psalmist said, "Love and faithfulness meet together; righteousness and peace kiss each other" (Ps. 85:10). Where do the two "kiss each other"? At the cross—that is God's great message of reconciliation and redemption. That is why Jesus could say, "My peace I give you" (John 14:27). He purchased it as the Righteous One dying on the cross.

Peace *must* be the fruit of righteousness. This is precisely why the Levitical priesthood was inadequate and that of Melchizedek effectual. As the priest of God, he is king of righteousness *and* peace. In this regard, Christ follows the order of Melchizedek, and because He alone *is* righteous, we can find peace only in Him.

To the king of righteousness and peace, "Abraham gave . . . a tenth of everything."

Melchizedek is without ancestry (v. 3). Melchizedek has no father, no mother, no genealogy, no recorded descendants. He was never born and he never died. In all of this, he was "like the Son of God" and, possibly most significant of all, his priesthood is "forever."

We can't be dogmatic as we scrutinize the evidence, but it appears as though Melchizedek was an Old Testament revelation of Jesus Christ. We do know that God viewed Abraham as His friend and frequently took him into His confidence. Paul tells us that God "announced the gospel in advance to Abraham" (Gal. 3:8). Was the bread and wine given to Abraham by Melchizedek merely for sustenance, or did it foreshadow the Last Supper in the upper room the night our Lord was betrayed?

The writer notes that in the Levitical priesthood the priests weren't able to continue "since death prevented them" (Heb. 7:23). Melchizedek, on the other hand, wasn't handicapped with such a problem. He "remains a priest forever" (Heb. 7:3). This suggests that he is currently functioning as our high priest. If Melchizedek and Christ aren't one and the same, it would appear that we have *two* high priests serving us in heaven.

Consideration of His Greatness — Hebrews 7:4-10.

> [4]Just think how great he was: Even the patriarch Abraham gave him a tenth of the plunder! [5]Now the law requires the descendants of Levi who become priests to collect a tenth from the people—that is, their brothers—even though their brothers are descended from Abraham. [6]This man, however, did not trace his descent from Levi, yet he collected a tenth from Abraham and blessed him who had the promises. [7]And without doubt the lesser person is blessed by the greater. [8]In the one case, the tenth is collected by men who die; but in the other case, by him who is declared to be living. [9]One might even say that Levi, who collects the tenth, paid the tenth through Abraham,

[10]because when Melchizedek met Abraham, Levi was still in the body of his ancestor.

Here we are introduced to a bit of Jewish logic. The writer concludes that Melchizedek's greatness over the Levitical priesthood is established by the fact that Abraham paid tithes to him. Let's follow his line of reasoning.

Levi (the ancestor of the priestly tribe) was Abraham's great-grandson. The record tells us that Abraham paid tithes to Melchizedek (Gen. 14). Therefore, it is reasonable to conclude that Levi paid tithes to Melchizedek, for he was Abraham's offspring, and "when Melchizedek met Abraham, Levi was still in the body of his ancestor" (Heb. 7:10). Levi, the priest who received tithes from the people, in turn paid tithes to Melchizedek through his great-grandfather Abraham. The conclusion is that Melchizedek is greater than Levi.

A keen appreciation for the logic of this argument may elude you, but one thing should strike home. What you are and do has repercussions for your descendants. Abraham's recognition of the supremacy of Melchizedek affected the life and ministry of Levi. *Because* Abraham gave tithes to Melchizedek, Melchizedek is better than Levi.

Whether you like it or not, you have been affected by your parents and grandparents, and you in turn will have a profound influence on your children and grandchildren.

The richness of our national heritage is the product of decisions made by our forefathers. We are deriving the benefits of their godly living and we in turn are setting the stage for future generations. Many embrace an ethic that allows for cheating, immorality, and compromising biblical absolutes, while steadfastly insisting that it makes no appreciable difference collectively as a nation. Such an argument merely acknowledges the truth that sowing in one generation is rarely reaped in the same generation. It is, however, unavoidably reaped some time in the future.

Just as the conduct of Abraham touched the life of Levi, so our conduct will certainly have repercussions for generations to come.

His Promise

The limitations of the Levitical system with its cumbersome laws and the inability of the priests to change the characters of the people showed the need for change. The very construction of the Old

Testament system was a temporary stopgap and promised such a change; and this is the subject of the next part.

Change Needed in the Old Order — Hebrews 7:11-19

[11]If perfection could have been attained through the Levitical priesthood (for on the basis of it the law was given to the people), why was there still need for another priest to come—one like Melchizedek, not like Aaron? [12]For when there is a change of the priesthood, there must also be a change of the law. [13]He of whom these things are said belong to a different tribe, and no one from that tribe has ever served at the altar. [14]For it is clear that our Lord descended from Judah, and in regard to that tribe Moses said nothing about priests. [15]And what we have said is even more clear if another priest like Melchizedek appears, [16]one who has become a priest not on the basis of a regulation as to his ancestry but on the basis of the power of an indestructible life. [17]For it is declared:

> "You are a priest forever,
> in the order of Melchizedek."

[18]The former regulation is set aside because it was weak and useless [19](for the law made nothing perfect), and a better hope is introduced, by which we draw near to God.

Mount Sinai was a watershed in Israel's history. It was one of the places where Moses and the delivered Israelites camped during the Exodus. While they were there, Moses met with God, and some fundamental changes were instituted.

Prior to Sinai there was no written law from God. Its presence was interwoven with the human conscience. Nor was there a priesthood with the accompanying altars and ritualistic rites. Each family offered their own sacrifices to God, the head of the family taking the place of a priest.

When Moses returned to the camp after having spent forty days with God on Mount Sinai, everything changed. God's law, an elaborate system of directives, was codified. Simply speaking, it can be broken into four major parts:

1. The moral law, which teaches us what God is like. In it, we see His unchanging nature revealed.

2. The ceremonial law, which prefigures the coming of Christ. In it, we have the priesthood, the sacrificial system, and the tabernacle and its accompanying furniture and accoutrements.

3. The cleansing law, which instructed the people in laws relating to disease, diet, and personal hygiene.

4. The civil law, which taught the people how to relate to one another. Much of this civil law is still included in modern societies despite the difference in political structure.

With this new law, God inaugurated the concept of a centralized priesthood. Gone were the days when the head of every household would offer sacrifices for his own family. The tribe of Levi was singled out for this privilege, and to the Levites each family brought its animal to be sacrificed.

It is important to note that both the law and the priesthood were instituted at Mount Sinai and in our passage in Hebrews we see the two inextricably linked. Their relation to one another is immediately apparent. In our sin, we have broken the commandments of God. The law revealed sin and exposed us for what we are—depraved people in need of redemption; the law shatters any delusion of self-righteousness that men might have. If we were perfect, we would have direct access to God without the need of a priest, but we are not perfect. We need a priest who will offer sacrifices to God in atonement for our sins.

Now, the law cannot save; its sole purpose is to expose our sins. Salvation, however, comes through the priesthood. The law revealed the problem; the priesthood revealed the solution.

Despite this truth, it soon became obvious to the Israelites that though the Levitical priesthood could *reveal* the solution, it could not *provide* it. Why the priesthood could not save people is the subject of verses 23-28. At this stage, we simply need to note the basic inadequacy of the Levitical priesthood.

The law instituted the Levitical priesthood, which in turn was incapable of making us righteous (perfect) before God (vv. 11-12). The solution to this problem is to be found in a new priesthood, but one not linked to the imperfection of the old order. To change the priesthood, the law needed to be changed, for the priesthood came as a result of the law.

The law stipulated that the priesthood was to come from the tribe of Levi (vv. 13-17). Jesus Christ, our High Priest, didn't come from the tribe of Levi, but from the tribe of Judah, a tribe that historically never served in the tabernacle. If Jesus had come from Levi, He would have been linked to an imperfect priesthood. With what priesthood then is He linked? As prophesied in Psalm 110:4, the priesthood of Melchizedek.

The law, like the Levitical priesthood was ineffectual, in that it could not render a person perfect before God (vv. 18,19). So the hope of the Old Testament was not seen in Sinai but in a brand new priesthood that could bring the people into a right relation with God.

Covenant Established by an Oath — Hebrews 7:20-22

> [20]And it was not without an oath! Others became priests without any oath, [21]but he became a priest with an oath when God said to him:
>
> "The Lord has sworn
> and will not change his mind,
> 'You are a priest forever.'"
>
> [22]Because of this oath, Jesus has become the guarantee of a better covenant.

The Levitical priesthood came into existence through the law. The priesthood of Jesus Christ came through a promise made by God on the basis of His unchanging love and grace and was not conditioned by our performance. This promise assures us of access to God (v. 19).

As if this were not enough, the writer underscores the fact that the Lord will not change His mind (v. 21). As if *that* were not enough, the promise itself assures us that Jesus Christ, following the order of Melchizedek, will be an eternal priest. There is not the slightest possibility of Jesus not reaching out and helping us with our problems.

His Performance

Figure 14 on page 95 contrasts Melchizedek with Levi and Christ with Aaron. Most of the chart is a review of what we have already learned in this section. In verses 1-3, we have no contrast; it is simply an introduction to the mysterious Melchizedek. In verses 4-10, the contrast with Abraham makes Melchizedek better than Levi. In verses 11-19, their contrasting relationship to *Sinai* means that Melchizedek is free from the imperfections of the law. Since Levi was imperfect, he could not make the people perfect; no one can make another perfect if he himself is imperfect. In verses 20-28, we have the differences between the two orders summed up for us.

Contrasting Abilities in the Priesthoods — Hebrews 7:23-25

> [23]Now there were many of those priests, since death prevented them from continuing in office; [24]but because Jesus lives forever, he has a permanent priesthood. [25]Therefore he is able

Figure 14

CONTRASTS BETWEEN THE TWO PRIESTHOODS

MELCHIZEDEK / CHRIST		LEVI / AARON	
Divisions in Chapter		Contrasts in Verses	
7:1-3	Who Melchizedek Was		
7:4-10	Received Tithes From Abraham	4	Paid Tithes to Melchizedek Through Abraham
	Gave a Blessing	6	Received a Blessing
	Lives Forever	8	Died
7:11-19	Free From an Imperfect Law	11	Married to an Imperfect Law
	Priesthood Unchanged by Virtue of His Life	12/ 16	Priesthood Changed by Virtue of His Tribal Heritage
	Could Make People Perfect	19	Could Not Make People Perfect
7:20-22	With an Oath	20	Without an Oath
7:23-25	One Priest	23/ 24	Many Priests
	Ever Liveth	23/ 24	Died
	Able to Save	25	Unable to Save
7:26-28	Separate From Sin	26/ 27	Sinner
	Offered Himself Once	27	Offered Sacrifices (animals) Many Times
	Perfect	28	Weak
	God/Man	28	Man

> to save completely those who come to God through him, because he always lives to intercede for them.

The Levites qualified for the priesthood on the basis of *outward* performance. They rigorously kept the law, dressed in the proper fashion, washed themselves according to certain forms, and carried out many other ceremonial requirements. Their pedigree had to be exact (coming from the tribe of Levi) and their outer consecration precise. But because of the shortcomings of their inner qualifications, it was necessary to have many of them; they constantly had to be replaced because of their sinfulness and subsequent death.

Jesus Christ, on the other hand, qualified for His priesthood on the basis of *inner* performance. Perfect in character, Jesus lives forever. (His priesthood will never change.) There is no need to worry about His successor. He Himself is the guarantee of this new and better covenant with God.

Christ's Sacrifice of Himself — Hebrews 7:26-28

> [26]Such a high priest meets our need—one who is holy, blameless, pure, set apart from sinners, exalted above the heavens. [27]Unlike the other high priests, he does not need to offer sacrifices day after day, first for his own sins, and then for the sins of the people. He sacrificed for their sins once for all when he offered himself. [28]For the law appoints as high priests men who are weak; but the oath, which came after the law, appointed the Son, who has been made perfect forever.

Once a year the faithful in Israel gathered before the tabernacle (or temple) for the Day of Atonement. It was a solemn occasion when the high priest entered the hallowed sanctuary, the Holy of Holies, through the veil separating it from the area of the Holy Place. Here in the somber gloom he sprinkled the sacrificial blood on the mercy seat of the ark of the covenant to make expiation for sin.

First to be sacrificed was a bullock, whose blood was brought into the Holy of Holies and sprinkled on the mercy seat by the high priest to make atonement *for his own sins.* Seven times with his fingers he would sprinkle the mercy seat. Then, returning to the hushed congregation he would sacrifice a goat and, taking its blood, would return to the Holy of Holies to repeat the sacred ritual, this time *for the sins of the people.*

It was necessary for the high priest "to offer sacrifices day after day, first for his own sins, and then for the sins of the people" (v. 27), "for the law appoints as high priests men who are weak" (v. 28). The sacrifices offered were ineffectual because the sacrifice of an animal could not pay the penalty for man's sins (see Heb. 10:4). An imperfect priesthood could offer only imperfect sacrifices.

What was needed was a perfect High Priest who could offer a perfect sacrifice. Man had sinned and so man had to pay the penalty for sin. So the perfect High Priest had to be a sinless man. The writer tells us we have such a high priest in Jesus Christ (Heb. 7:26). As the perfect Man, He could offer the perfect sacrifice, and that He did when He offered Himself. This is what the cross is all about: "He himself bore our sins in his body on the cross" (1 Peter 2:24).

As the conqueror of death, He continues to function as our High Priest in heaven, for His priesthood is "made perfect forever" (Heb. 7:28). His ministry of atonement being complete, He is now engaged in a continual ministry of intercession.

Referring once again to Figure 13 on page 78, we see that because Jesus Christ is after the order of Melchizedek, He is not limited by the law given at Sinai nor by the limitations of the sacrificial system. In verses 1-10 we saw that Christ perfected the priesthood through His person (who He was), bringing with Him a *Better Order*. Verses 11-22 revealed the promise (why He came), which was to bring a *Better Covenant*. Finally, in verses 23-28, we see our Lord's performance (what He did), when He became a *Better Priest*.

The priesthood of Christ, linked to the order of Melchizedek, and therefore not limited by the Old Testament sacrificial system, is a *perfect* one. As a Christian you can relax, for . . .

- You don't have to pay for your sins —He did.
- You don't have to offer sacrifices —He did.
- You don't have to look for a better priest —He is perfect.
- You don't have to look for someone to intercede for you before God —He does.
- You have been liberated to enjoy a fulfilled life in thankful service to God.

Jesus Himself put it this way: "I have come that they may have life, and have it to the full" (John 10:10).

HEBREWS 8:1–13

Figure 15

THE PLACE OF CHRIST'S MINISTRY

(His Is a Better Covenant)

Hebrews 8

BETTER MINISTRY		BETTER MEDIATOR	BETTER COVENANT	
8:1-5		8:6	8:7-13	
Contrasting Ministries		MEDIATOR	Contrasting Covenants	
Christ's High Priesthood	Levitical High Priesthood		New Covenant	Old Covenant
Perfect Sacrifice	Imperfect Sacrifice		Written on Hearts	Written on Stones
Perfect Priest	Imperfect Priest		Superior - Grace	Inferior - Law
Heavenly Tabernacle	Earthly Tabernacle		Unconditional	Conditional
Real	Shadow		Faultless	Found Fault

7

THE PLACE OF CHRIST'S MINISTRY

Having studied this far in the Epistle to the Hebrews, could you summarize in a sentence or two your thoughts on its message? How would you word it? At the beginning of this section, the writer gives us his summary of the previous seven chapters by saying, "The point of what we are saying is this: We do have such a high priest, who sat down at the right hand of the throne of the Majesty in heaven, and who serves in the sanctuary, the true tabernacle set up by the Lord, not by man" (Heb. 8:1-2).

In the first half of this book, the writer has placed the emphasis on the *person* of Jesus Christ. In chapters 1–2, he shows that Christ is better than angels, first in His divinity and then in His humanity. In chapters 3–4, he proves that Jesus is better than Moses, in that through Him we have access to God with the rights and privileges of heirs to the throne. In chapters 5–7, we see that our Lord follows the high priestly order of Melchizedek, providing through His perfection the assurance of our salvation.

In chapter 8, the author switches the emphasis to the *ministry* of Jesus Christ. Now, it goes without saying that the *person* and *ministry* of our Lord are inseparably linked; what a person does is determined by who the person is.

The ministry of our Lord Jesus is better than the ministry of the Old Testament priesthood for the simple reason that it is established on a better covenant. The author's subject in chapter 8 is this *covenant,* then in chapters 9 and 10 he shows how this covenant allows Christ to administer a superior ministry.

This chapter divides itself into three parts, with verse six serving as a pivotal section all on its own. With reference to Figure 15 on page 100, we have as our outline:

- A Better Ministry (vv. 1-5)
- A Better Mediator (v. 6)
- A Better Covenant (vv. 7-13)

A *better ministry* established on a *better covenant* has been made possible by the ministry of the *better Mediator,* Jesus Christ.

A Better Ministry — *Hebrews 8:1-5*

> [1]The point of what we are saying is this: We do have such a high priest, who sat down at the right hand of the throne of the Majesty in heaven, [2]and who serves in the sanctuary, the true tabernacle set up by the Lord, not by man.
>
> [3]Every high priest is appointed to offer both gifts and sacrifices, and so it was necessary for this one also to have something to offer. [4]If he were on earth, he would not be a priest, for there are already men who offer the gifts prescribed by the law. [5]They serve at a sanctuary that is a copy and shadow of what is in heaven. This is why Moses was warned when he was about to build the tabernacle: "See to it that you make everything according to the pattern shown you on the mountain."

We are brought into the throne room of the Most High God, and there we observe that after enduring so ignominious a death, our Lord Jesus is now enthroned at the right hand of God the Father, in the place of supreme honor and exaltation. This was possible for Jesus because of who He is, and in His perfection, death could not keep Him (Heb. 7). In His perfection it was not necessary to offer a sacrifice for Himself. In His perfection, He unselfishly gave His life for our sins and so became our High Priest forever. In His perfection, a sacrifice for sin never needs repeating; never again will payment for our sins need to be made. His was an absolute atonement.

So we see Him here in His glory (v. 1). But He continues to function as our High Priest. We are then told that even in His glorification, Jesus continues to minister (v. 2). This reminds us of His words while He was on earth: "For even the Son of Man did not come to be served, but to serve, and to give his life a ransom for many" (Mark 10:45).

He is King, but He is also Priest. Jesus' kingship is in terms of service not majesty. In this truth we find an example and an application for our own lives.

We encounter many forms of promotion and honor during our lives. Advancement, whether in business, in an organization, or in the military, is one form. Retirement is another, in that it consists of pay without work. How do you respond when these things come your way? Do you sit back expecting to be served? Or do you look around you to see how your new position can enable you to serve others better? Is your mental attitude *I served long and hard to get this promotion and now it's my turn to be served?* Or are you following the example of our Lord Jesus?

Jesus too served long and hard to get to the throne. His was a life where He was constantly being misunderstood and rejected. He gave repeatedly and without the pleasure of being appreciated in return. The anguish of hell and the cross were His. But now we see Him "At the right hand of the throne of the Majesty in heaven." And what is His posture? That of a servant. Exalted, the attitude of our Savior is *Now I have an even better opportunity to serve!*

Jesus' ministry is summarized for us in verses 3-4. Its context is as follows: (for a sinful person) there is no access to God apart from sacrifice. The prophet Ezekiel put it succinctly when he said, "The soul who sins is the one who will die" (Ezek. 18:20). Earthly priests are limited in that they can offer only imperfect sacrifices: "Because it is impossible for the blood of bulls and goats to take away sins." (Heb. 10:4). In contrast to this, our Priest, Jesus Christ, not limited by the Levitical system, is not on earth but in heaven, having offered the perfect sacrifice. "But when this priest had offered for all time one sacrifice for sins, he sat down at the right hand of God. . . . because by one sacrifice he has made perfect forever those who are being made holy" (Heb. 10:12,14).

The writer then quotes from the Pentateuch, and in so doing touches on *why* God instituted the Levitical system at Mount Sinai (Exod. 25:40). Because this is the subject of chapter 9, we will defer dealing with it exhaustively at the present time. Before moving on, however, we would do well to weigh carefully the Word of God quoted in verse 5. God legislated that the code of religion He was instituting was to be adhered to rigidly; He was not prepared to tolerate the smallest degree of syncretism. It was extremely important that the Hebrews should not bring into their worship of God any alien ideas, irrespective of their origin. For example, they were forbidden to borrow forms or rituals from the pagan religions around them, and when they did, they found themselves in deep trouble, as illustrated by Israel at the time of the divided kingdom. It all began with the northern kingdom (Israel) establishing alternative places for worship, since Jerusalem was part of the southern kingdom (Judah). This seemingly harmless move paved the way for still more changes, and eventually culminated in Israel's worshiping the iniquitous gods of the Canaanites.

For 20th-century man, the application of Exodus 25:40 relates not so much to the physical trappings that accompany worship, but more to the current arena of "ideas." It is fashionable today to bring into question certain biblical teachings such as divorce, the place of women in the church, and the doctrine of hell. What is stated clearly in Scripture is now becoming the target for open attack. Satan was the first to raise the question, "Hath God said . . . ?" (see Gen. 3) and men have been following his example ever since.

That we will be influenced by our environment is inevitable, but we must be steadfastly committed to keeping our worship of God free from extrabiblical ideas, however intrinsically "reasonable" or "appealing" they may appear.

A Better Mediator — *Hebrews 8:6*

> [6]But the ministry Jesus has received is as superior to theirs as the covenant of which he is mediator is superior to the old one, and it is founded on better promises.

This verse stands by itself in a pivotal position, providing a bridge between the first and third sections of chapter 8. Looking again at Figure 15 on page 100, we see in verses 1-6 *contrasting ministries* and in verses 6-13 *contrasting covenants*. As Jesus' ministry is greater than the Levitical ministry, so Jesus' covenant is greater than the Old Testament (Old Covenant). It was His superior ministry that enabled Him to be the mediator of a superior covenant.

This is represented graphically on the bottom section of the chart under the *contrasting ministries,* tying the ministry and mediation of Christ together, and under *contrasting covenants,* tying the covenant and mediation of Christ together.

Christ's High Priesthood is greater than the *Levitical high priesthood* just as the *new covenant* is greater than the *old covenant.* The *perfect sacrifice* of Christ is greater than the *imperfect sacrifice* of the

Old Testament, just as the new covenant was *written on the heart* whereas the old covenant was *written on stone* (and so forth through the chart).

All these comparisons hinge on the work of Jesus Christ as our Mediator. We note again that as Jesus' ministry is greater than the Levitical ministry, so Jesus' covenant is greater than the Old Testament (Old Covenant).

Another sense in which Jesus Christ stands in a pivotal position is that He is the Savior in both the Old and the New Testaments. To explore this truth more fully will help us gain a more complete understanding of verses 7-13. Look at Figure 16.

Figure 16

JESUS AS MEDIATOR AT THE CENTER OF HISTORY

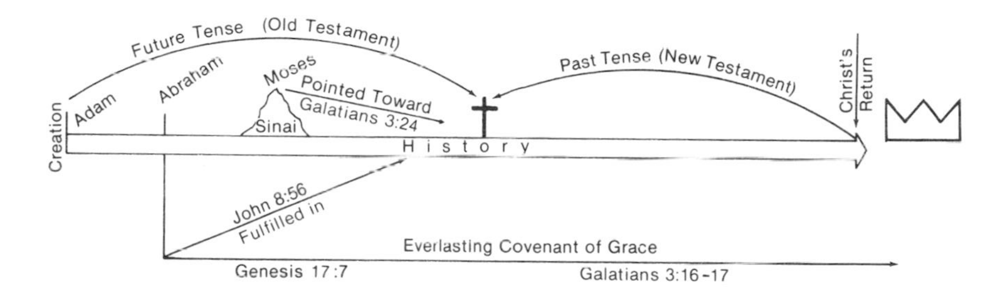

The Bible views history as being linear rather than circular. History, according to the Bible, has a definite beginning and a definite end, the latter being when God will consummate human history with the return of Christ.

Man's entrance into history began with Adam, who then disobeyed God and was responsible for the problem of sin in the human race. Though it is not clear how it originated, the concept of sacrifice was introduced early in human history (Gen. 4). One is led to believe that it was linked to the promise of redemption given by God at the Fall:

"And I will put enmity between you and the woman, and between your offspring and hers; he will crush your head, and you will strike his heel" (Gen. 3:15).

Abraham is the next man to appear on our line of history. His life is important for several reasons. He was the first Hebrew and thus the father of Israel. An unconditional promise was given to him and his descendants, which was both *gracious* and *everlasting*. We represent this by drawing a line under the line of history and parallel to it showing that it was in effect during this passage of time. This unconditional promise was given to Abraham several times (see Gen. 12; 15; 17). It is clearly stated in this promise: "I will establish my covenant as an everlasting covenant between me and you and your descendants after you for the generations to come, to be your God and the God of your descendants after you" (Gen. 17:7).

Moses is the next person included in our line of history. He is called "the great law giver" because of his encounter with God on Mount Sinai during the Exodus from Egypt. It was there that Israel ratified a covenant of condition.

> "'Now if you obey me fully and keep my covenant, then out of all nations you will be my treasured possession. Although the whole earth is mine, you will be for me a kingdom of priests and a holy nation.' These are the words you are to speak to the Israelites." So Moses went back and summoned the elders of the people and set before them all the words the Lord had commanded him to speak. The people all responded together, "We will do everything the Lord has said." So Moses brought their answer back to the Lord (Exod. 19:5-8).

Note the word *if*. This reveals a condition. God said, "*If* you will do . . . *then* I will do. . . ." Right after Israel's ratification, God gave part of the condition—the Decalogue (Exod. 20). Before Moses could return to the camp with this word from God, however, the people of Israel had already broken it (see Exod. 32).

Moses then interceded on behalf of the people, making no mention of the conditional covenant entered into about forty days before, but referring to the unconditional covenant made with Abraham centuries earlier. "Remember your servants Abraham, Isaac and Israel, to whom you swore by your own self: 'I will make your descendants as numerous as the stars in the sky and I will give your descendants all this land I promised them, and it will be their inheritance forever.' Then the Lord relented and did not bring on his people the disaster he had threatened" (Exod. 32:13-14).

The promise given to David (2 Sam. 7:13-15) and to others along the line of history simply elaborates and clarifies the form that the covenant would take.

Why then do we call it a *new* covenant? (Heb. 8:8). The *new* is contrasted with the *old* in that the latter is based on what I do to earn heaven (keep the law) as opposed to the former, which is based on what Christ does for me. The *old* is conditional; the *new* is unconditional. The *new* is grace; the *old* is law. Actually, the *new* was given before the *old,* in that Abraham came before Moses. But the Abrahamic covenant found its fulfillment in Jesus Christ, and for this reason it is called the *new covenant.*

The *old covenant* of the law could never save. No one but Jesus has ever kept the law perfectly. Only the *new covenant* can save. Salvation is a gift of God, an expression of His grace made possible by the sacrificial death of Jesus Christ in payment for our sins. Knowing that the Abrahamic covenant was linked inextricably to Himself, Jesus said, "Your father Abraham rejoiced at the thought of seeing my day; he saw it and was glad" (John 8:56).

Every person on the line of history (Figure 16, page 105) was saved by the *new covenant* of grace. It was fulfilled at the cross. Those in the Old Testament were saved by looking forward in expectation *(future tense)* and we in the New Testament are saved by faith in Him who has come *(past tense).*

A Better Covenant — *Hebrews 8:7-13*

[7]For if there had been nothing wrong with that first covenant, no place would have been sought for another. [8]But God found fault with the people and said:

"The time is coming, says the Lord,
when I will make a new covenant
with the house of Israel
and with the house of Judah.
[9]It will not be like the covenant I made with
their forefathers
when I took them by the hand to lead
them out of Egypt,
because they did not remain faithful to my covenant,
and I turned away from them,
declares the Lord.
[10]This is the covenant I will make with the
house of Israel
after that time, says the Lord.
I will put my laws in their minds

and write them on their hearts.
I will be their God,
and they will be my people.
[11]No longer will a man teach his neighbor,
or a man his brother, saying, 'Know the Lord,'
because they will all know me,
from the least of them to the greatest.
[12]I will forgive their wickedness,
and will remember their sins no more."

[13]By calling this covenant "new," he has made the first one obsolete; and what is obsolete and aging will soon disappear.

The "first covenant," or the old covenant, had "fault" written all over it (review Heb. 7:11-28). This was the covenant that God made with Israel through Moses (Heb. 8:9). Because of its limitations, God promised a new covenant (v. 8, as quoted from Jer. 31:31-34). Let's take a closer look at what is said in this passage.

This covenant is shown to be *inner* rather than *outward* (Heb. 8:10-12). That is, the accent is on what God will do *in* us rather than on how we perform. Forgiveness (v. 12) is a gift of God. It is not earned by our good behavior or outward deeds. *God* is going to take His laws and inscribe them on our hearts. *He* is going to be merciful to us in our unrighteousness and *He* will remember our sins no more.

We find that there is something disturbing about these verses as we probe their significance. In a sense, we can identify with their fulfillment in Christ, but in a sense we cannot. For example, is this statement really true? "No longer will a man teach his neighbor, or a man his brother, saying, 'Know the Lord,' because they will all know me, from the least of them to the greatest" (v. 11). Or again, what does he mean that the old "will soon disappear" (v. 13)? Is he suggesting that it is still here?

A new "line of history" with the cross in the center may help clarify the problem (Figure 17). In a certain sense, the old covenant was not completely abolished at the cross. True, at that time the sacrifice of animals ceased and everyone had the opportunity of access to the presence of God (we no longer need a human priesthood). But there are parts of the old covenant that still linger (see v. 11). We still need teachers and not "all" know the Lord.

The new covenant found its fulfillment in Jesus Christ, but we who are in New Testament times experience a "fading" of the old and a blossoming of the new. Only after Jesus returns again will the old covenant be entirely discarded.

Figure 17
THE RELATIONSHIP OF THE OLD AND THE NEW COVENANTS

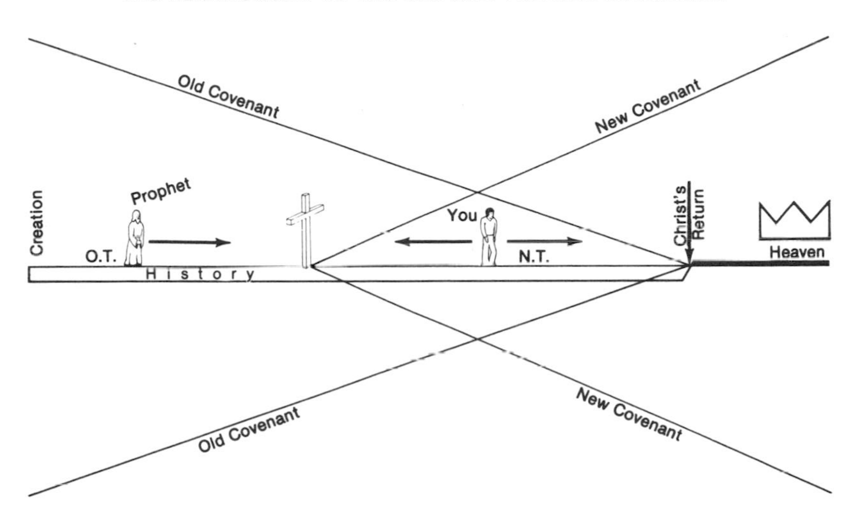

A clear illustration of this may be seen in Peter's address at Pentecost (Acts 2). In it, he quotes from the Prophet Joel (2:28-32), including the section "And I will show wonders in the heaven above and signs on the earth below, blood and fire and billows of smoke. The sun will be turned to darkness and the moon become as blood before the coming of the great and glorious day of the Lord" (Acts 2:19-20). Though part of the new covenant, this part of Joel's prophecy has yet to see its fulfillment. It relates to the climactic fulfillment of the new covenant, brought about by Jesus' return.

At the cross, the new covenant was fulfilled, but not all of the *old* left, and not all of the *new* came. Though fulfilled, it is still in the process of being worked out.

Another truth worth viewing, as we study this passage as illustrated by Figure 17, has to do with the sort of perspective the Old Testament prophets had. An illustration may help you grasp this: Close one eye and line up two pencils in front of you so that they appear as one. Imagine that the closest pencil represents the first advent of Christ and the other pencil the second advent. From where the Old Testament prophet stood in history, these appeared as one.

Figuratively speaking, we stand in the New Testament between the two pencils. The first advent of Christ is history; the second advent of our Lord is yet to be realized some time in the future.

When we read the Old Testament, therefore, we must keep this difference in mind. For example, the Joel passage that Peter quoted at Pentecost views the two advents as one. Another case of this may be seen when Jesus was reading from Isaiah during a service at the synagogue in Nazareth. Isaiah had recorded, "The Spirit of the Sovereign LORD is on me, because the LORD has anointed me to preach good news to the poor; He has sent me to bind up the broken-hearted, to proclaim freedom for the captives and recovery of sight for the prisoners, to proclaim the year of the LORD's favor and the day of vengeance of our God" (Isa. 61:1-2). As you read the Luke account, however, you notice that Jesus stopped reading after the words, "to proclaim the year of the Lord's favor" (Luke 4:18,19). He left out the rest, "and the day of vengeance of our God." After closing the Book of Isaiah, Jesus declared, "Today this Scripture is fulfilled in your hearing" (Luke 4:21).

What Jesus read (Isa. 61:1-2a) refers to the first advent; the rest of the prophecy (v. 26), to the second advent. To Isaiah they appeared as one.

"What is obsolete and aging will soon disappear" (Heb. 8:13). The old Levitical order instituted by Moses is obsolete, having been superseded by Jesus Christ. The writer of Hebrews again reminds his readers of the folly of returning to the old system, no matter how attractive the circumstances.

The old Mosaic system was an economy of legalism and self-effort. Following it led to defeat and discouragement. Jesus has delivered us from our entrapment. To return to a system that is decaying and enslaves in the process is at best a tragic mistake. Yet how easy it is to slip into its seemingly attractive clutches.

Trying to establish a relationship with God or seeking His forgiveness through self-effort or "works" is a sure sign that one is heading in that direction. So also is the establishment of *any* rule that is not in the Bible with the suggestion that others must follow it. Such thinking is ruinous; it wears the clothes of decay and death.

We can live in a new economy that is fresh with the fragrance of Jesus Christ. Having tasted of His grace and freedom, let us not return to the old system.

HEBREWS 9:1—10:18

Figure 18

THE PRIESTLY MINISTRY OF CHRIST

(His Is a Better Sacrifice)

Hebrews 9:1 - 10:18

Better Tabernacle		Better Blood			Better Sacrifice		Better Remission	
Old Tabernacle Inadequate	Christ the New Tabernacle	Necessity of Blood:	To Ratify Old Covenant	To Redeem in The New Covenant	Purpose of Old Sacrifice	Promised New Sacrifice	Forgiveness Found in Christ	Promised in Old Testament
9:1-10	9:11-12	9:13-17	9:18-22	9:23-28	10:1-4	10:5-10	10:11-14	10:15-18

OLD COVENANT

REMINDER OF SIN

PURPOSE OF *SHADOW*

1. Inadequacy of Man's Way
2. Picture of God's Way

NEW COVENANT

REDEMPTION FROM SIN

PURPOSE OF *REAL*

1. Delivered From Sin
2. Reconciled to God

8

THE PRIESTLY MINISTRY OF CHRIST

During my wife's aunt and uncle's Pacific cruise, we met their magnificent luxury liner in one of its port stops. After a delightful day of enjoying one another's company, we were relaxing in the ship's lounge. The atmosphere was idyllic—a beautiful sunset, worthy of a tropical paradise, and in the background the orchestra's melodic strains mingling fluently with the laughter and chatter of the other passengers.

Surveying the scene, my wife asked, "Are these people really as happy as they appear?" "Oh, no," her aunt replied, "not if those I've talked to are representative of the group."

Purpose, meaning, and reality are qualities of life so desperately sought after by people and, judging by results, so difficult to obtain. Yet Jesus said, "I have come that they may have life, and have it to the full" (John 10:10). Ushering in a rich, full, abundant life was the purpose of our Lord's coming to earth. He came to bring a touch of reality to otherwise empty lives. Nowhere in Scripture is this more clearly seen than in this Epistle to the Hebrews. It presents the Old Testament system as merely a shadow of the real, as is the case of every person's life before it is invaded by the Savior. In both instances, it is Jesus who brings reality.

The reader has already been introduced to this concept: "They serve at a sanctuary that is a copy and *shadow* of what is in heaven"

(Heb. 8:5). In this section, we find these statements: "This is an *illustration* for the present time" (Heb. 9:9); "the *copies* of the heavenly things" (Heb. 9:23); and the writer again calls our attention to this theme in saying, "The law is only a *shadow* of the good things that are coming—not the *realities* themselves" (Heb. 10:1).

These three words are all meant to connote the same thing—shadow, illustration, and copy. What the writer is saying is that the "real" is in heaven and the "shadow" here on earth (see 2 Cor. 5:1-2). That which God instituted on Mount Sinai with Moses was merely an "illustration" of the work of Christ, signifying to Israel at the time what lay in store.

My wife enjoys sewing, and it is not uncommon for me to see bits of paper pinned to material scattered on the table. Those bits of paper, the "pattern," are invaluable in helping her make the garment. They give her the exact shape the individual pieces of material should be. They fulfill this function perfectly, but can never be assembled to substitute for the garment itself. I have never seen my wife dress in the "pattern." It serves a purely utilitarian function for her. The finished garment, however, is worn often.

The Levitical system was never intended to bring reality. That is as futile as thinking that reality and fulfillment can be achieved through self-effort, whether that self-effort be in the form of asceticism, hedonism, or something in between. Only in Jesus Christ can true reality be acquired, and all else is valid only as it brings us into an encounter with Him.

From this, we can draw several conclusions:

1. The worship we offer to God is but a pale reflection of the true worship enjoyed in heaven. Our forms and "aids to worship" are no more "the real" than were the accompaniments of the tabernacle. Putting your trust or seeking fulfillment in form, liturgy, or institutions can only lead to disappointment.

2. This truth assists our understanding the difference between the universal church and the local church. Hopefully, the local congregation is but a "shadow" of the heavenly congregation. At least, this is a goal toward which all believers should strive.

3. In this distinction between "copy" and the real, we see the purpose of the Old Testament system. God inaugurated the Levitical order with the sacrifices and the tabernacle to give us a preview of the coming attractions in Jesus Christ.

The Old Testament people were not perfected by the Old Testament system. The shadow can never make perfect; only the real can do this. What the shadow can do, however, is to let us know that the real is just around the corner. The Old Testament showed that we needed a better tabernacle, a better blood, a better sacrifice, and a better means to have our sins forgiven; and this we find in the person of Jesus Christ (note Figure 18 on page 112). He came to perfect the people. He did this by providing a . . .

- Better Tabernacle (9:1-12)
- Better Blood (9:13-28)
- Better Sacrifice (10:1-10)
- Better Remission (10:1-18)

A Better Tabernacle

As we have already seen, the old tabernacle built at the foot of Mount Sinai was inadequate in meeting the needs of the people. What was needed was a totally new tabernacle, constructed by the hand of God rather than by the hand of man. Such a tabernacle is to be found in Jesus Christ, and this is the subject of the first part.

The Old Tabernacle Was Inadequate — Hebrews 9:1-10

[1]Now the first covenant had regulations for worship and also an earthly sanctuary. [2]A tabernacle was set up. In its first room were the lampstand, the table and the consecrated bread; this was called the Holy Place. [3]Behind the second curtain was a room called the Most Holy Place, [4]which had the golden altar of incense and the gold-covered chest of the covenant. This chest contained the golden jar of manna, Aaron's rod that had budded, and the stone tablets of the covenant. [5]Above the chest were the cherubim of the Glory, overshadowing the place of atonement. But we cannot discuss these things in detail now.

[6]When everything had been arranged like this, the priests entered regularly into the outer room to carry on their ministry. [7]But only the high priest entered the inner room, and that only once a year, and never without blood, which he offered for himself and for the sins the people had committed in ignorance. [8]The Holy Spirit was showing by this that the way into the Most Holy Place had not yet been disclosed as long as the first tabernacle was still standing. [9]This is an illustration for the present time, indicating that the gifts and sacrifices being offered were not able to clear the conscience of the worshiper. [10]They are only a matter of food and drink and various ceremonial washings—external regulations applying until the time of the new order.

Figure 19

THE HEBREW TABERNACLE AND ITS FURNITURE

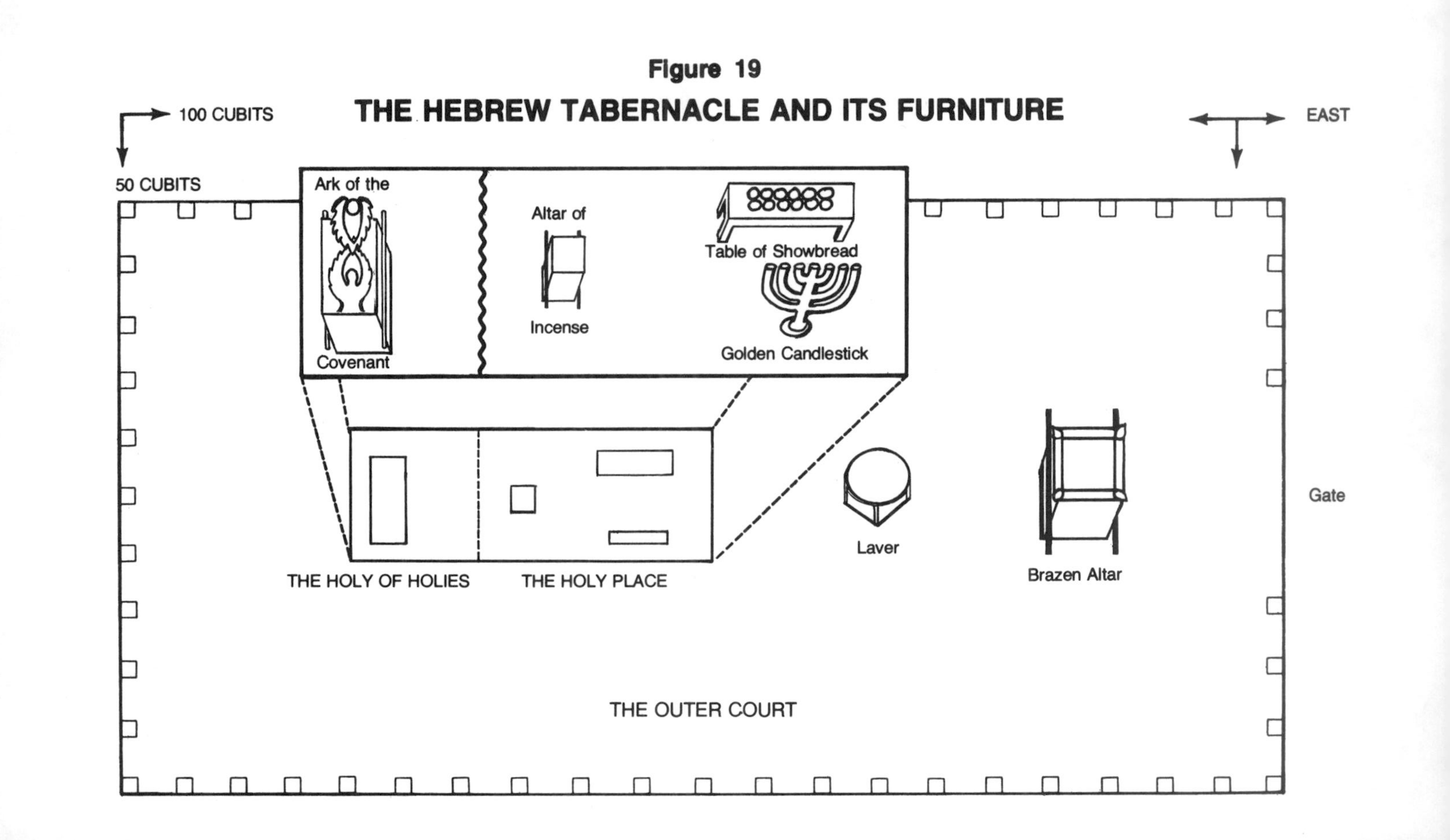

The passage begins by enumerating the "furniture" of the Holy Place and the Holy of Holies (vv. 1-5). Simply drawn, it looks like Figure 19 on page 116. The dimensions were originally given in cubits, an ancient unit of length based on the distance from the elbow to the tip of the middle finger, about 18 inches.

First there was the outer court, which was 100 by 50 cubits or 150 feet long by 75 feet wide. Only the Levites could come into this court. The rest of the people were required to observe the proceedings from the outside.

Surrounding the outer court was a wall 7½ feet high, made of white linen (symbolizing purity and holiness). The 30-foot-wide entrance faced the east. Israel had just left Egypt, where the sun played a central role in indigenous religion and worship. Lest the people confuse God with the worship of the sun, the Levites entered the tabernacle to offer the morning sacrifice from the east, with the sun to their backs.

The first item in the outer court was the brazen altar. It was 7½ feet square, 4½ feet tall, and made of acacia wood overlaid with brass. The top had a grating and each of the four corners had a horn to which the animal was tied. Two sacrifices were offered every day—morning and evening—with many more on Israel's special days.

The next thing to be observed as one walked across the outer court was the laver, where the priests ceremonially washed themselves. Made of polished brass (the kind used by women for mirrors), it was where the priests went through the rites of purification.

Dominating the court was a rectangular tent, called the tabernacle. The overall dimensions were 30 x 10 cubits, or 45 x 15 feet. The first and largest section of the tabernacle was the sanctuary, or Holy Place, into which only the priests were permitted to go in their tabernacle service. The inner section was called the Holy of Holies and here only the high priest was permitted to enter, and then only on the Day of Atonement.

The Holy Place contained three items of furniture. First, on the right, as one entered, was the table of showbread. It was 3 feet long, 1½ feet wide, and made of acacia wood overlaid with gold. Every sabbath twelve freshly baked loaves of bread (two rows of six, representing the twelve tribes of Israel) were placed on the table. This "bread of presence" was deemed holy and was only to be eaten by the priests.

On the south side of the sanctuary was the seven-branched candlestick. It was fashioned out of solid gold, and pure olive oil was burned in it night and day.

Right in front of the veil guarding the Holy of Holies was the altar of incense—1½ feet square; it also was made of acacia wood overlaid with gold. The burning incense symbolized the people's prayers rising to God.

Beyond the veil was the Most Holy Place, the Holy of Holies. In it stood the ark of the covenant. Like some of the other vessels, this too was made of acacia wood and lined inside and out with gold. Resting on top of the ark was the mercy seat, and on the mercy seat stood two cherubim facing one another. Each cherub had one wing stretched over the mercy seat, while covering himself with the other. It was here, above the mercy seat, that God's presence abode.

Stored inside the ark of the covenant were a "golden pot" carrying a sample of the manna that God used to feed the people during the Exodus, Aaron's rod that budded, and the stone tablets of the law engraved by the finger of God on Mount Sinai. On one occasion, there was a dispute in Israel regarding who could function as priest (Num. 17). God had ordained the tribe of Levi, whereas for years the head of each household had served in that capacity. To substantiate the fact that the Levites' claim had originated with God, Moses got each tribe to place an almond rod before the ark of the covenant. The next day only Aaron's rod budded, and this took "away their murmurings."

Separating the Holy of Holies from the Holy Place was a veil. It was this veil (in New Testament times found in Herod's temple) that was rent in two at the death of Christ on the cross (see Luke 23:45). This signified that the Levitical priesthood had come to an end and all people could now freely enter God's presence at any time.

The reason that access into the Holy of Holies was limited was to reveal that the Levitical system could not reconcile a person to God (Heb. 9:8). This is the first of the weaknesses of the Old Testament priesthood mentioned.

The second weakness was its inability to reach home to the conscience (v. 9). The ceremonies could only cleanse the outer man. These interrelated shortcomings had to wait for their resolution till "the time of the new order," the time when God would set things right through Christ.

Christ the New Tabernacle — Hebrews 9:11-12

[11]When Christ came as high priest of the good things that are

> already here, he went through the greater and more perfect tabernacle that is not man-made, that is to say, not a part of this creation. [12]He did not enter by means of the blood of goats and calves; but he entered the Most Holy Place once for all by his own blood, having obtained eternal redemption.

The new tabernacle was able to do for us what the old tabernacle could not—provide redemption. This new tabernacle is the body of Christ Jesus. In these two verses, three key words catch our attention.

Came—Jesus came as our high priest. "But we see Jesus, who was made a little lower than the angels, now crowned with glory and honor because he suffered death, so that by the grace of God he might taste death for everyone" (Heb. 2:9). The purpose of His coming was to die and thereby satisfy the wrath of God against our sins.

Entered—Jesus entered, not the Holy of Holies in Herod's temple, for that was "man-made," but into heaven itself—the real Holy of Holies—to pay the penalty for our sins.

Obtained—When Jesus entered the Holy of Holies in heaven, it was to obtain "eternal redemption" for us.

He came, He entered, He obtained—these are the three aspects of Jesus' sacrifice of Himself. Jesus *came* to earth to die that He might *enter* the presence of God and *obtain* our redemption by paying for our sins. The price our Savior paid for our redemption was His blood. Mentioned twice in this passage, blood becomes the subject of the rest of the section.

Better Blood

Moses recorded God saying that "the life of a creature is in the blood, and I have given it to you to make atonement for yourselves on the altar; it is the blood that makes atonement for one's life" (Lev. 17:11). Blood is the key ingredient in the sacrifice as it is brought to God in payment for sin. For God said, "The life of the flesh is in the blood."

This is an important concept in biblical Christianity, yet rarely discussed. The average believer hears a sermon on the subject of blood infrequently. Perhaps it is because many feel it is a gory concept, a trifle barbaric.

Actually, it is a wonderful concept, not one at all from which we should shy away. Many of the great hymns of the faith refer to the "blood of the Lamb" and to the idea of being "washed in the blood." The writer of Hebrews refers to it no fewer than twelve times in this passage. We are saved, says the writer, by the *blood* of Jesus Christ.

The Necessity of Blood — Hebrews 9:13-17

> [13]The blood of goats and bulls and the ashes of a heifer sprinkled on those who are ceremonially unclean sanctify them so that they are outwardly clean. [14]How much more, then, will the blood of Christ, who through the eternal Spirit offered himself unblemished to God, cleanse our consciences from acts that lead to death, so that we may serve the living God!
>
> [15]For this reason Christ is the mediator of a new covenant, that those who are called may receive the promised eternal inheritance—now that he has died as a ransom to set them free from the sins committed under the first covenant.
>
> [16]In the case of a will, it is necessary to prove the death of the one who made it, [17]because a will is in force only when somebody has died; it never takes effect while the one who made it is living.

The writer refers here to the blood of goats and calves which was offered only on the Day of Atonement as already explained (v. 12). We see this expanded to include other types of sacrifice (v. 13). Certain acts, like coming in contact with a dead person, required ceremonial cleansing, which was accomplished by the offering of sacrifices. But all this merely touched the outward man. How is the inner man changed?

Our Lord Jesus pinpointed the problem in a conversation with the Pharisees, when He said, "Don't you see that whatever enters the mouth goes into the stomach and then out of the body? But the things that come out of the mouth come from the heart, and these make a man 'unclean.' For out of the heart come evil thoughts, murder, adultery, sexual immorality, theft, false testimony, slander. These are what make a man 'unclean'; but eating with unwashed hands does not make him 'unclean'" (Matt. 15:17-20).

This "inner defilement" was untouched by animal sacrifice. Only the blood of Christ could do that (Heb. 9:14); His blood "cleansed our consciences from acts that lead to death." The problem of the conscience was introduced earlier (v. 9) and here the solution is presented (v. 14). The conscience is purged from *dead works* (KJV), that is, all those expressions of self-effort that cannot solve the problem of guilt (see Heb. 6:1). You feel guilty because you are guilty, and only the blood of Christ can cleanse you and take your guilt away.

Notice the contrast between the death of the animals and the death of Christ (vv. 13,14). Christ offered Himself, something no animal was ever able to do. The Old Testament high priest knew the significance of the animal being sacrificed, but the animal did not. With Jesus the opposite was true. Those who killed Him did not know what they did. It was Christ the sacrifice who was fully aware of the import of His act.

The necessity of blood is seen in the use of the word *redemption* (v. 15), which can also be translated "ransom." S & H Green Stamps used to be a familiar sight to many people. When several books of these stamps had been collected, they were taken to a redemption center and exchanged for household goods or the like. To redeem them, was to "buy back."

As sinners, we are in bondage and are servants of unrighteousness. Our sins offend the holiness of a perfect God. Again and again God has communicated that "the wages of sin is death" (Rom. 6:23). For God to "wink" at our sins and restore fellowship with us without demanding that the wages of sin be paid mocks His Word and makes Him a liar. Enslaved to sin, we need to be *ransomed.*

The price of sin is death, but life is found in the blood. Jesus' blood was shed to pay the penalty of our sins and buy us back from bondage. *God paid the ransom to Himself in order to satisfy His justice and assure us that He means what He says.* He does not take sin lightly.

Next we come to the role of a will or testament (vv. 15-17). At least two observations can be made from this section: 1) A will or testament comes into force only after the death of the one making it. Payment of the inheritance can be made only after the death of the testator. For believers to inherit eternal life, the one who bequeathed this life to us, Jesus Christ must first die. 2) Jesus' death was retroactive for those who died during Old Testament times. Those under the first (old) testament who put their trust in God also became heirs of eternal life, even though they died *before* the testator. It was as though these people were saved on *credit.*

In summary, notice the use of the word *eternal* in this passage:

- Verse 12—eternal redemption—this was the purpose of Christ's coming.
- Verse 14—eternal Spirit—the means by which God redeems us.
- Verse 15—eternal inheritance—the result of Jesus' work for us.

To Ratify the Old Covenant — Hebrews 9:18-22

[18]This is why even the first covenant was not put into effect

without blood. [19]When Moses had proclaimed every commandment of the law to all the people, he took the blood of calves, together with water, scarlet wool and branches of hyssop, and sprinkled the scroll and all the people. [20]He said, "This is the blood of the covenant, which God has commanded you to keep." [21]In the same way, he sprinkled with the blood both the tabernacle and everything used in its ceremonies. [22]In fact, the law requires that nearly everything be cleansed with blood, and without the shedding of blood there is no forgiveness.

The writer of Hebrews again refers us back to the Mosaic covenant instituted at Mount Sinai and reminds us that even this testament was inaugurated with blood. Referring back to Siani (see Exod. 24), he says, "In fact, the law requires that nearly everything be cleansed with blood, and without the shedding of blood there is no forgiveness" (Heb. 9:22).

To *ratify* is to approve, sanction, or confirm. God will not ratify a relationship with man without blood. This was true at the beginning of human history after the sin of Adam, for we see immediately following the Fall the introduction of sacrifice (Gen. 4). Though the blood of animals could not pay the penalty for man's sins, it was a constant reminder to man that God's justice had to be satisfied.

Most people seek to minimize the importance of their sins. They try to suppress guilt by dwelling on the good deeds they have done. When reminded that they are sinners, they water down the gravity of this fact by referring to sin as a "weakness" or calling it by some other name. If this fails, they take refuge by either blaming others or suggesting that such "shortcomings" are their own business.

This is possibly one of the reasons "enlightened" people don't like the concept of blood as a strong feature in their theology. It is a reminder of the awfulness of sin. Sin, no matter how trivial it may appear to the offender, cannot be casually shrugged off. The shedding of blood makes it clear that the forgiveness of sin is not something to be treated lightly.

The forgiveness that God extends to us is a costly thing. The blood of animals was used to ratify the old covenant; the blood of Christ redeems in the new covenant. In either case, "without the shedding of blood there is no forgiveness" (v. 22).

To Redeem in the New Covenant — Hebrews 9:23-28

[23]It was necessary, then, for the copies of the heavenly things to be purified with these sacrifices, but the heavenly things themselves with better sacrifices than these. [24]For Christ did not

enter a man-made sanctuary that was only a copy of the true one; he entered heaven itself, now to appear for us in God's presence. [25]Nor did he enter heaven to offer himself again and again, the way the high priest enters the Most Holy Place every year with blood that is not his own. [26]Then Christ would have had to suffer many times since the creation of the world. But now he has appeared once for all at the end of the ages to do away with sin by the sacrifice of himself. [27]Just as man is destined to die once, and after that to face judgment, [28]so Christ was sacrificed once to take away the sins of many people; and he will appear a second time, not to bear sin, but to bring salvation to those who are waiting for him.

The old covenant was a copy "of the heavenly things." It was not the real but a shadow of the real. The Old Testament system and its ceremonial ratification with blood was simply a "preview of the coming Christ." The preview was shown over and over again as the years passed into centuries. But the actual "event" happened only once. In this passage we see the finality of Christ's sacrifice. The contrast is made between "often" and "once." Note the contrasts between men and Christ in Figure 20.

Figure 20

Men		Christ
entered a man-made tabernacle	verse 24	entered heaven
offered blood often	verse 25	offered blood once
offered blood of others	verse 25	offered His own blood
made many sacrifices	verse 26	made one sacrifice
are sinful	verse 26	put away sin
die once and are judged	verses 27, 28	died once for salvation

Better Sacrifice

Blood, death, suffering, sacrifice—all are related to one another in that they are involved in making payment for our sins. Though blood and sacrifice are closely allied, the emphasis of the previous section (Heb. 9) is on the former, while the latter occupies center stage in the passage we are about to consider.

The Purpose of the Old Sacrifices — Hebrews 10:1-4

> [1]The law is only a shadow of the good things that are coming—not the realities themselves. For this reason it can never, by the same sacrifices repeated endlessly year after year, make perfect those who draw near to worship. [2]If it could, would they not have stopped being offered? For the worshipers would have been cleansed once for all, and would no longer have felt guilty for their sins. [3]But those sacrifices are an annual reminder of sins, [4]because it is impossible for the blood of bulls and goats to take away sins.

Once again the writer reverts to the theme mentioned earlier: "A shadow of what is in heaven" (Heb. 8:5). A shadow is not without value, for it is cast by something with substance. The presence of the shadow promises the presence of the substance.

The purpose of the law in general and the sacrificial system in particular was twofold:

First, *to show the inadequacy of man's way*. The sacrifices offered year by year can never make people perfect (v. 1). "Now there were many of those priests, since death prevented them from continuing in office" (Heb. 7:23). "The Holy Spirit was showing by this that the way into the Most Holy Place had not yet been disclosed as long as the first tabernacle was still standing" (Heb. 9:8). "But those sacrifices are an annual reminder of sins" (Heb. 10:3). They could repeat their ritualistic observances as often as they liked, but such observances could never solve the problem of man's alienation from God.

Second, *to give a picture of God's way*. "The law is only a shadow of the good things that are coming" (v. 1), "copies of the heavenly things" (Heb. 9:23), and "an illustration for the present time" (Heb. 9:9). Every aspect of the Levitical system was rich in meaning as it portrayed the function of Christ. Each and every act symbolized some facet of our Lord's ministry.

The conscience is again the subject here ("felt guilty," v. 2, see Heb. 9:9,14). The sacrifice of animals, like the blood of animals simply could not purge people from sin. The key thought and one that was no doubt forgotten by people in the Old Testament as well as in the New Testament is here expressed: "Because it is impossible for the blood of bulls and of goats to take away sins" (v. 4). The reader could easily accuse the Book of Hebrews of redundancy on this subject, but that is only because we are *studying* it. It becomes an entirely different question when translated into everyday life. Then it is easy to allow this cardinal truth to get out of focus.

For the Jews to whom this letter was written, this blurring of vision happened when they as Christians reverted to Judaism in the face of persecution. For us, it may show in having a benign attitude toward non-Christian religions, believing that "though our way may be best, there is good in all the religions of the world." Such an attitude may be correct if we are merely searching for an ethic by which to live. If, however, we are grappling with how sinful man can be reconciled to a holy and just God, this is an entirely different matter.

Realizing that he has his hands on one of the rarest and most precious diamonds in the Scriptures, the writer of Hebrews allows us the privilege of examining its many facets.

Man sinned. Removal of the problem requires payment for that sin. Each person may pay for his own sin, but the very act of paying results in eternal separation from God. Man is incapable of solving his dilemma. People in the Old Testament saw this in the frequency of their animal sacrifices; we in the New Testament era see it in the propitious death of Jesus Christ.

The Promised New Sacrifice — Hebrews 10:5-10

5Therefore, when Christ came into the world, he said:

"Sacrifice and offering you did not desire,
but a body you prepared for me;
6with burnt offerings and sin offerings
you were not pleased.
7Then I said, 'Here I am—it is written about
me in the scroll—
I have come to do your will, O God.'"

8First he said, "Sacrifices and offerings, burnt offerings and sin offerings you did not desire, nor were you pleased with them" (although the law required them to be made). 9Then he said, "Here I am, I have come to do your will." He sets aside the first to establish the second. 10And by that will, we have been made holy through the sacrifice of the body of Jesus Christ once for all.

Further proof that the Levitical system of sacrifice could not take away sin is seen in Psalm 40:6-8, quoted here with commentary added (Heb. 10:5-9). The psalm is, of course, referring to Jesus Christ. In this messianic promise we see that God clearly told the people that the blood of bulls and goats cannot take away sin. Only a human body would satisfy for sin.

The argument here is simply this: God disavowed any recognition that animal sacrifice could serve as payment for sin (Ps. 40:6). Next He says, "Here I am, I have come . . . to do your will, O my God" (Ps. 40:7, 8). The "I" refers to a person (the Messiah), and not to an animal. He comes to do the will of God, that is, that which animal sacrifices could not do—pay for our sins. So we see in the Old Testament a promise (not the only promise) regarding the Messiah's propitious work.

In these opening verses of chapter 10 we can see the contrasts between the old sacrifices and the New Sacrifice (see Figure 21).

Figure 21

Animals	Jesus
They had no choice. An expression of law	He chose to die. An expression of love
We pay our debts because we *have* to. We give a gift because we *want* to.	
They did not think. Mechanical sacrifice	Jesus was rational. Moral sacrifice

Better Remission

We come now to the climax of Jesus' redemptive work. Reiterated for us are two great truths: First, His once-for-all sacrifice has broken down all the barriers that existed between us and God; second, it achieves all that was promised in the Old Testament.

Forgiveness Found in Christ — Hebrews 10:11-14

> [11]Day after day every priest stands and performs his religious duties; again and again he offers the same sacrifices, which can never take away sins. [12]But when this priest had offered for all time one sacrifice for sins, he sat down at the right hand of God. [13]Since that time he waits for his enemies to be made his footstool, [14]because by one sacrifice he has made perfect forever those who are being made holy.

The completed work of Christ (vv. 12-14) is contrasted with the futility of the Levitical priest's ritual. The writer makes us take a retrospective look at these men who performed the same act day after day, an act pathetically incapable of transforming the inner man. An analogy could easily be drawn with one of the Eastern religions, *except* for the fact that in the Old Testament the practice performed by the priests was never intended to be anything more than an image foreshadowing the real.

Even the sacrifice of the high priest on the Day of Atonement was insufficient. "Day after day every priest stands and performs his religious duties; again and again he offers the same sacrifices, which can never take away sins" (v. 11). The very fact of such repetition magnified the problem and stimulated in the heart of the believer a longing for a permanent solution to his dilemma.

Our great High Priest terminated the old order with His once-for-all sacrifice at Calvary. Having offered the perfect sacrifice, however, Jesus did not cease to be our High Priest. The writer reasons that just the opposite is true. Because He "offered for all time one sacrifice for sins," He is eligible to be our High Priest throughout eternity (v. 12). There is no longer a place for repeated sacrifice, but the need for intercession remains.

Spiritually, Jesus is present everywhere, indwelling the life of every believer. Physically, He is at the right hand of God (v. 12). Next comes a picture of triumph (v. 13). His victory over sin and death assures the ultimate subjugation of every evil force.

Remove sin, forgiveness, remission, perfection, our sanctification all speak of the same thing. It is now possible for sinful people to be reconciled to a holy and righteous God. Our acceptance by God is neither partial nor temporary. We are assured that we are "perfect" in God's sight, and that "forever." Our sins—no matter how great their atrocity—have been *paid in full* by the all-sufficient sacrifice of Christ. We are forgiven, not by a capricious act of God that can as easily be rescinded, but by a carefully thought-through and costly act of self-sacrifice by the Godhead, thus completely irrevocable in its character.

Forgiveness Promised in the Old Testament — Hebrews 10:15-18

[15]The Holy Spirit also testifies to us about this. First he says:

[16]"This is the covenant I will make with them
after that time, says the Lord.

I will put my laws in their hearts,
and I will write them on their minds."

[17]Then he adds:

"Their sins and lawless acts
I will remember no more."

[18]And where these have been forgiven, there is no longer any sacrifice for sin.

Through his Epistle, the writer quotes profusely from the Old Testament Scriptures. The truths he has outlined, therefore, are not his ideas; they are rooted in what the Holy Spirit has revealed in "the Law and the Prophets." "The Holy Spirit says" attests to the fact that the Scriptures view themselves as being divinely authored.

Here again the writer quotes Jeremiah (31:31-34; see Heb. 8:8-12). A different point is being made, however. Earlier, the writer was showing that the new covenant found in Jesus Christ replaced the old Mosaic covenant (chapter 8). The old was in the process of decay and was being replaced by the new.

Here he is making the same basic point that he made in verses 12-14, showing that ready access to God by all believers was promised in the Old Testament. It was not a new idea introduced by Jesus or those close to Him. The heart of the whole Old Testament Scriptures pulsates in expectation of this event. Jeremiah talked about forgiveness and the remission of sin (v. 17), and the writer of Hebrews concludes that this mighty privilege becomes possible when there is no longer a need for animal sacrifices (v. 18).

The old and new covenants had a great deal in common, but they led to different goals. Refer to the bottom section of Figure 18 on page 112. Both covenants had a tabernacle, a high priest, blood, sacrifice, and cleansing in common. The old system provided a reminder of sin with a twofold purpose: to show the inadequacy of man's way and to give a picture of God's way. The new system secured redemption from sin with its twofold purpose: deliverance from sin and reconciliation to God. The old covenant pointed to the *Cross*. The new covenant points to the *crown*.

"There is no longer any sacrifice for sin" (v. 18). With these words, the writer brings to an end the account of the priesthood of Christ and with it the first section of Hebrews. In the rest of the book, the reader is exhorted to apply what he has learned and received. And well might he be. Having pondered the price of our redemption, the believer is both humbled and motivated to a life of commitment.

What language shall I borrow
  To praise Thee, heavenly Friend,
For this Thy dying sorrow,
  Thy pity without end?
Lord, make me Thine forever,
  Nor let me faithless prove;
O let me never, never
  Abuse such dying love.*

*"O Sacred Head" by Paul Gerhardt.

HEBREWS 10:19–39

THE ENDURANCE OF FAITH

Hebrews 10:19-39

Figure 22 **"Since we . . . have confidence . . . do not throw away your confidence."**

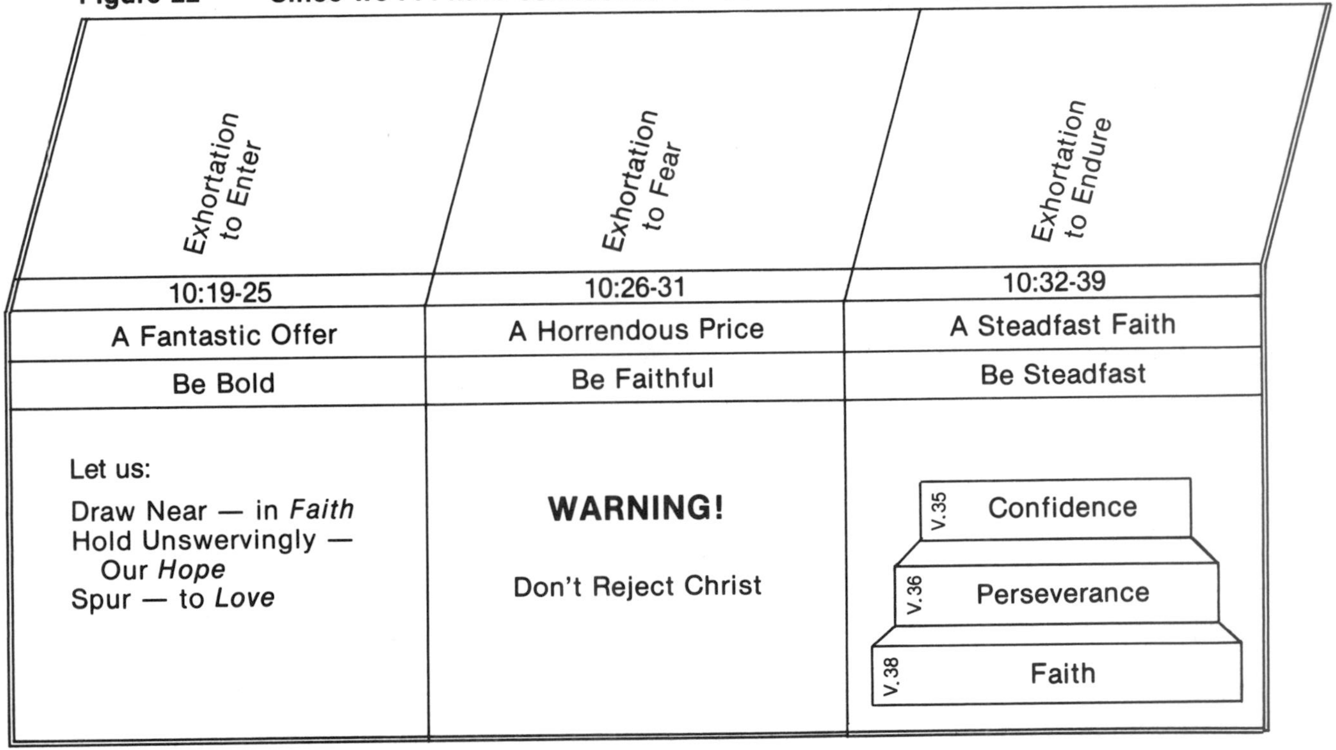

Exhortation to Enter	Exhortation to Fear	Exhortation to Endure
10:19-25	10:26-31	10:32-39
A Fantastic Offer	A Horrendous Price	A Steadfast Faith
Be Bold	Be Faithful	Be Steadfast
Let us: Draw Near — in *Faith* Hold Unswervingly — Our *Hope* Spur — to *Love*	**WARNING!** Don't Reject Christ	V.35 Confidence V.36 Perseverance V.38 Faith

9
ENDURANCE OF FAITH

A life of faith is the natural result of appropriating for oneself the efficacious work of Jesus Christ. By its very nature, a sacrifice of the magnitude described in the previous chapters demands absolute commitment from us, its beneficiaries. This is the subject of the remaining portion of the Book of Hebrews (see Figure 1 on page 8).

The writer begins his discourse on the subject of faith with an exhortation to *endure*. God makes a promise, then we act on that promise and anticipate certain results. But what happens if the results are not apparently forthcoming? We have committed ourselves by faith. Will God keep His side of the bargain? Yes, our writer assures us, for "you need to persevere so that when you have done the will of God, you will receive what he has promised" (Heb. 10:36). In the meanwhile you must endure patiently.

Such an experience is not unique. Satan would have us believe that our problems and temptations are unique, but that is not the case. Paul assured the Corinthians, "No temptation has seized you except what is common to man" (1 Cor. 10:13). And the writer of Hebrews provides us with an opportunity to stand in review of the Old Testament saints who had problems (Heb. 11). There we see the *examples and explanation of faith*. Many of them "were still living by faith when they died. They did not receive the things promised; they only saw them and welcomed them from a distance. And they admitted that they were foreigners and strangers on earth'' (Heb. 11:13).

How easy it is to become ''weary in doing good.'' Everything in us wants to quit or at least slow down. We cannot afford such a luxury, warns the writer (Heb. 12). Those who fought the battles in former days are now in the grandstands watching us who are still in the arena. With our eyes on Jesus, we must ''throw off everything that hinders and the sin that so easily entangles, and let us run with perseverance the race marked out for us'' (Heb. 12:1). This section describes the *encumbrances of faith.*

Finally, we must also consider the *expressions of faith* (Heb. 13), the ''basics'' of the Christian life. Included in the list are such things as love, visiting those in prison, and entertaining strangers. These are rather difficult to do when under persecution, and that ''stranger'' just may be an enemy, but such is the life of faith.

It was in desperation that John and Mary first embraced Jesus Christ as their Savior and Lord. Their fragile world had begun to crumble. Circumstances for which they had made no allowance began to invade their lives. Mary's father had just died, and they had always been close.

To furnish their modest home after marriage had meant buying on time. Then John fell victim to a massive layoff at the plant. With John unable to make payments, one by one their possessions were reclaimed by their creditors.

About this time, some friends introduced them to a home Bible study, which began to quicken some dormant ideas they had learned in Sunday school as children. ''So this is what the gospel is all about,'' confided John to his wife. ''If Jesus loves us *that* much and is willing to straighten out our lives, we'd be fools to turn down His offer.'' So they turned their lives over to the Savior.

But John didn't get his job back right away. Not only that, Mary had a miscarriage and the resulting operation meant they would never have children. ''Where was Jesus when all of this happened?'' groaned John in a tone that verged on being cynical. ''I thought He was supposed to *help* us when we got into trouble.''

This young couple came to grips with a problem that has confronted believers from the days of Job. What does it mean for us to have a High Priest in heaven? What practical difference can we expect it to make in our lives? Christians are not immune to the seeming tragedies of life; often they seem to have more than their fair share. Can it be that we are actually having *more* difficulties in our lives as Christians than we did before we turned to Christ?

The Jewish Christians, to whom the Book of Hebrews was addressed, had similar questions in their minds. When hunted like wanted criminals *because* they were believers, the constricting Law of Moses didn't look so bad after all. The temptation to resort to Judaism was very strong.

But the writer is adamant. Not only is *Christ the Perfect High Priest* (Heb. 1:1–10:18), but *Christ* is also *the Perfect Way* (Heb. 10:19–13:25), trials and difficulties notwithstanding. Referring to Figure 22 on page 132, the passage before us may be summarized by the words "Since we have confidence . . . do not throw away your confidence" (Heb. 10:19,35). The three divisions are:

- Exhortation to Enter (10:19-25)
- Exhortation to Fear (10:26-31)
- Exhortation to Endure (10:32-39)

Exhortation to Enter — *Hebrews 10:19-25*

[19]Therefore, brothers, since we have confidence to enter the Most Holy Place by the blood of Jesus, [20]by a new and living way opened for us through the curtain, that is, his body, [21]and since we have a great priest over the house of God, [22]let us draw near to God with a sincere heart in full assurance of faith, having our hearts sprinkled to cleanse us from a guilty conscience and having our bodies washed with pure water. [23]Let us hold unswervingly to the hope we profess, for he who promised is faithful. [24]And let us consider how we may spur one another on toward love and good deeds. [25]Let us not give up meeting together, as some are in the habit of doing, but let us encourage one another—and all the more as you see the Day approaching.

The most sacred and at the same time the most mysterious part of the Hebrew tabernacle was the Holy of Holies. Situated in the back of the sanctuary, a large, forbidding veil gave the cubicle an ominous appearance. Only the high priest could step behind it, and then only once a year.

How awesome, then, it must have been for those priests on duty that first Good Friday. No sooner had Jesus cried out, "It is finished," and died, than that huge tapestry tore from top to bottom (Matt. 27:51). Wondering if they should hide or risk a hesitant look, the priests must have simply stood there rooted to the ground with their mouths agape.

At that moment, the Holy of Holies lost its sanctity. It had been superceded by "a new and living way . . . that is, His body" (Heb. 10:20). No longer was the entrance into the Holy of Holies the exclusive right of the high priest. It now became the inclusive right of every believer—regardless of sex, age, position, or race—to enter.

As the veil in the Old Testament tabernacle was the only way into the Holy of Holies, so the veil of Jesus' flesh is the only entrance into the presence of God. Though this is a review of what has already been said, it is imperative that the believer who is subjected to untoward circumstances, remind himself of this great truth time and again: Jesus provides the *only* access to God.

The *exhortation to enter* is a call to action—action that is with confidence and assurance. The three pivotal words to consider are *faith* (v. 22), *hope* (v. 23 [translated as faith in the KJV]), and *love* (v. 24).

Draw Near in Faith — v. 22

This is a *call to worship* based on the sacrifice of Christ. The wording here is analogous to that concerning the Old Testament rites of purification, only this time the inner man is made clean. The idea of conscience comes before us once again, for our hearts have been cleansed from an evil conscience.

Our experience tends to deny this as we consider our sins and selfishness. We feel unclean and guilty when we contrast our lives with that of Jesus Christ. The more mature we become in Christ, the worse this problem becomes. The closer we get to the Savior, the sharper the contrast between Him and us and the more unworthy we feel. This is why early in his ministry Paul said, "I am the least of the apostles" (1 Cor. 15:9); later he stated, "I am less than the least of all God's people" (Eph. 3:8); and at the end of his life he declared himself to be the worst of sinners (1 Tim. 1:15). Did the great apostle become *less* sanctified through the years? No, he came progressively closer to Jesus and felt increasingly unworthy. This is sanctification.

This is why it requires faith to draw near to the Lord. We feel guilty and unworthy, but Jesus says our consciences are cleansed. We must jump the hurdle of our emotions and "by faith" enter boldly into His presence.

Hold Unswervingly to Our Hope — v. 23

This is *a call* to *confess* to a hostile world the object of our faith. The "confession of our hope" has to do with what we believe. Faith and confession are welded together. Notice how Paul combined them: "If you confess with your mouth, 'Jesus is Lord,' and believe in your heart that God raised him from the dead, you will be saved. For it is with your heart that you believe and are justified, and it is with your mouth that you confess and are saved" (Rom. 10:9-10).

The reason the believer doesn't "confess" to others isn't that he is timid, though it is often disguised as such. We can talk to people about a large range of subjects, such as the weather, business, world affairs, and sports. A reluctance to talk to others about Christ is usually related to a fear of being rejected. Add to this that the people to whom the letter was written were being oppressed for their commitment to Christ, and it is easy to empathize with their reluctance.

Given these circumstances, what does the writer encourage them to do? "Hold unswervingly to the hope we profess."

Spur One Another Toward Love — v. 24

This is *a call to proper conduct.* These fearful, harassed believers were not only exhorted to witness, but to *congregate* with fellow believers (v. 25). Common sense would seem to dictate that the best plan under such circumstances would be to scatter and pretend you didn't know other Christians. It would seem that gathering together, no matter how surreptitiously, would be inviting disaster.

It was for precisely this reason, however, that they needed to be strengthened by one another. The mutual encouragement and exhortation to good works is often most needed when we least feel like doing good works. For so many of us, a desire to be a recluse is a sure sign that we need the fellowship of other believers. It is a time of carrying "each other's burdens" (Gal. 6:2).

When our family was going through the agony of losing our oldest son to leukemia, in my heartache I wanted to withdraw and be alone. Yet it was our Christian friends who surrounded us with their love and prayers, and buoyed us up, helping us through our crisis.

In summary, the statement "let us draw near" deals with the *heart* and has to do with our relation to God. "Let us hold unswervingly" deals with the *mouth* and has to do with our relation to the world. "Let us . . . spur" deals with our *conduct* and has to do with the church.

Exhortation to Fear — *Hebrews 10:26-31*

[26]If we deliberately keep on sinning after we have received the knowledge of the truth, no sacrifice for sins is left, [27]but only a

fearful expectation of judgment and of raging fire that will consume the enemies of God. [28]Anyone who rejected the law of Moses died without mercy on the testimony of two or three witnesses. [29]How much more severely do you think a man deserves to be punished who has trampled the Son of God under foot, who has treated as an unholy thing the blood of the covenant that sanctified him, and who has insulted the Spirit of grace? [30]For we know him who said, "It is mine to avenge; I will repay," and again, "The Lord will judge his people." [31]It is a dreadful thing to fall into the hands of the living God.

This fourth warning is similar to Hebrews 6:4-6 in that these are two of the most misunderstood passages in the Bible. Some would suggest that the writer is teaching that it is possible to lose your salvation by deliberately sinning (v. 26). The context simply does not bear this out. We can see this in Figure 23.

Figure 23

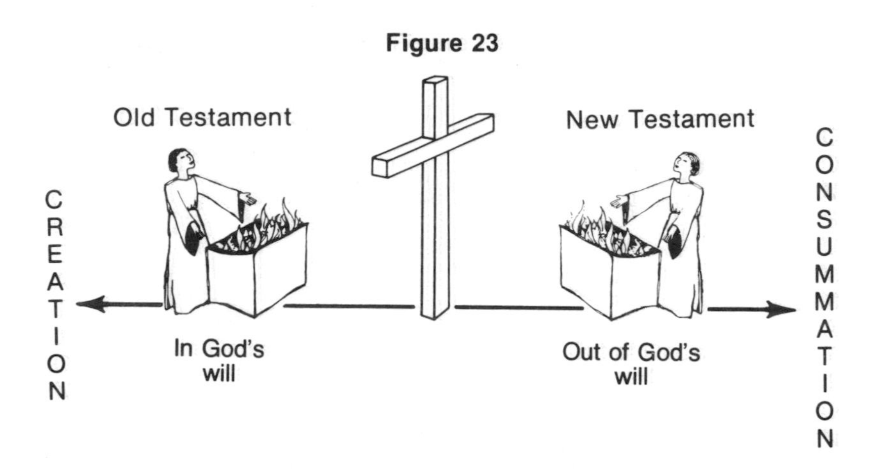

Again we draw the line of history with the cross in the center. Let us say we lived during the time of Christ. Now, Jesus died on the cross on Friday. Would it have been proper to offer sacrifice on the Saturday (Sabbath) *before* the crucifixion? "Yes," you answer correctly, "for it is done in anticipation of the Messiah's sacrifice for us" (see Isa. 53). What about the other days leading up to Good Friday? Yes, for the same reason. Now let us jump to the Monday *after* Good Friday. Is it now proper to offer sacrifice? No, for God's perfect sacrifice has already been offered. The day before Christ's death we sacrifice in the will of God; the day after, out of God's will.

With this in mind, we can now apply our illustration to the problem of this warning. Several years have now transpired since the cross. Living in some far-flung corner of the Roman Empire, some Jews had not heard and understood what had happened at Calvary. The writer spent a considerable portion of his letter explaining it (Heb. 1:1–10:25). To trust in animal sacrifices in anticipation of the Messiah, even though He had already come, was excusable. But to continue trusting in them, having properly understood the cross, is a wilfull rejection of Christ's sacrifice.

For such people who "deliberately keep on sinning after [they] have received the knowledge of the truth, no sacrifice for sins is left, but only a fearful expectation of judgment and of raging fire that will consume the enemies of God" (Heb. 10:26,27). Their actions are tantamount to having "trampled the Son of God under foot," having "treated as an unholy thing the blood of the covenant that sanctified [them], and having "insulted the Spirit of grace" (v. 29).

This passage, to be understood properly, must be interpreted in its historical setting. The application, however, is the same for us today as it was for the original recipients. If we reject Christ's sacrifice in payment for our sins, there is no other provision for our salvation (v. 26).

Jesus Christ will come twice and only twice. The first advent was for the purpose of going to the Cross. He became a man and "suffered death, so that by the grace of God he might taste death for everyone" (Heb. 2:9). The second advent will be for judgment (see Heb. 10:27).

We have already been warned that judgment awaits us on the other side of death (Heb. 9:27). Now we are told that "it is a dreadful thing to fall into the hands of the living God" (Heb. 10:31). In our introduction, we saw five warnings sprinkled through the book. This one is the fourth: *don't reject Christ!*

Don't reject the salvation God has offered to you. Don't procrastinate. Don't talk yourself into believing that God will give you a "second chance" after you die, or that there is no such thing as "judgment" and "raging fire." Once again God warns us on this subject. It is not an issue with which we can trifle.

If, as you read this, you are aware that there has never been a time in your life when you have transferred allegiance from yourself to Jesus Christ and trusted His propitious death to cover your sins, or if you are *unsure* if you have ever done this, then put this book down right now and open your heart to God in prayer, receiving Jesus as your Savior and Lord.

If you are unsure of what to say, simply pray, "Lord Jesus, I recognize that I am a sinner. I am unworthy of eternal life and recognize that nothing I can do will earn it. I confess that because of my sin I am worthy of Your wrath. Thank You for dying for my sins. Forgive my sins. Come into my life and change me. Make me Your child. I ask this in Your most holy name. Amen."

Exhortation to Endure — *Hebrews 10:32-39*

[32]Remember those earlier days after you had received the light, when you stood your ground in a great contest in the face of suffering. [33]Sometimes you were publicly exposed to insult and persecution; at other times you stood side by side with those who were so treated. [34]You sympathized with those in prison and joyfully accepted the confiscation of your property, because you knew that you yourselves had better and lasting possessions.

[35]So do not throw away your confidence; it will be richly rewarded. [36]You need to persevere so that when you have done the will of God, you will receive what he has promised. [37]For in just a very little while,

"He who is coming will come and will not be late.
[38]But my righteous one will live by faith.
And if he shrinks back,
I will not be pleased with him."

[39]But we are not of those who shrink back and are destroyed, but of those who believe and are saved.

Earlier, the exhortation was *to enter,* since we have access into God's presence "by a new and living way" (Heb. 10:19-25). Next, the exhortation was *to fear,* lest in the turbulence of difficulties we are tempted to retreat to our former manner of life (vv. 26-31). Now the exhortation is *to endure,* remembering that the object of our confidence is not the pleasure of the world but the promises of God. The passage suggests that there is a fivefold secret to enduring. The key words in this secret are *exhort, fellowship, remember, hope,* and *faith.*

1. *Exhort* (v. 24)—"Spur one another toward love and good deeds." When you see another Christian in difficulty, go to him and draw him into your love. Encourage him with your love and prayers and exhort him to hold fast.

2. *Fellowship* (v. 25)—Do "not give up meeting together." Related to the first point, the exhortation here is to surround yourself with Christian friends when the going gets rough. Don't be a loner. Share your burdens with others and let them help carry the load.

3. *Remember* (v. 32)—"Remember those earlier days." Throughout the Old Testament, God admonishes His people to remember. Remember all that God has done for you; review how God has led; retrace the footsteps of God in your life; keep a spiritual diary of God's leading. Then when the difficulties and problems arise, draw strength and encouragement from it.

4. *Hope* (v. 37)—"He who is coming will come and will not be late." Hope is also the subject earlier when the writer said, "And all the more as you see the Day approaching" (v. 25). This, of course, speaks of the second coming of Christ. The day is coming when God will consummate human history in the person of Christ. The apostle Paul said, "I consider that our present sufferings are not worth comparing with the glory that will be revealed in us' " (Rom. 8:18).

5. *Faith* (v. 38)—"My righteous one will live by faith." This great quote is central to both the epistles to the Romans and Galatians (Hab. 2:4; see Rom. 1:17; Gal. 3:11). It speaks of faith in God and His promises. Paul also said, "Just as you received Christ Jesus as Lord, continue to live in him" (Col. 2:6). We *live* in Jesus the same way we *received* Him—by faith.

Note that the situation is described first (Heb. 10:32-34), then the promise is given (vv. 35-39). Outwardly, the situation appears to be catastrophic. The afflictions of these people were great (v. 32); ridicule and shame dogged their heels (v. 33); their possessions were plundered and ransacked (v. 34).

What can the Christian conclude from this bleak situation? Negatively, God never promised that life would be easy, nor that our circumstances would be more appealing than the circumstances of those who don't believe in Christ.

Positively, we are promised Christ's presence (v. 19), that we have in heaven "better and lasting possessions" (v. 34), that doing the will of God does have its reward (v. 35,36), that Jesus will come again (v. 37), and that our souls will be saved (v. 39).

All of this is not to be construed to mean that life is a disaster from which one longs to escape, and that if only one holds on long enough, life will be over and we can go to heaven. The promises of God pertain to *both* this life and the life to come.

In this life, both the believer and the non-Christian experience heartaches and disappointments. But there the similarity ends. Unlike the non-Christian, the believer has the presence of God in His life, giving him strength and encouragement. He is able to place his difficulties in a broader perspective, giving them purpose and meaning (though he doesn't always understand what the purposes are), and he recognizes that reality is not to be found in this life alone. On the other side of the grave is a life absent of sin, suffering, and heartache, for it is in the very presence of God.

Again referring to Figure 22 on page 132, we see that foundational to all of this is *faith,* which becomes the subject of the next chapter. Built on this foundation is *endurance,* which has to do with hanging on when the going gets rough. Faith builds endurance and endurance builds *confidence.* When we don't endure, but turn back when confronted by adversity, our confidence is shattered. This is what happened to the Israelites at Kadesh Barnea (the subject of Heb. 3–6).

Here, then, is a summons to persevere, to never be less than our best. Our confidence is not in circumstances, but in God and His ability to turn them to ultimate good.

HEBREWS 11:1–40

Figure 24

EXPLANATION AND EXAMPLES OF FAITH

Hebrews 11:1-40

Explanation of Faith	Examples of Faith		Exploits of Faith	
Definition	The Patriarchs	The Exodus and the Conquest	Deliverance From Persecution	Deliverance Through Persecution
11:1-3	11:4-22	11:23-31	11:32-35a	11:35-40
Definition	Demonstration		Deliverance	
Purpose	Promises		Persecution	

FAITH IS OBEYING THE PROMISES OF GOD

Faith	Promises	Obedience
Guarantee of the Future Proof of the Invisible	Faith Without a Promise Isn't Faith — It Is Presumption 2 Peter 1:4	Promises Without Obedience Isn't Faith — It Is Unbelief John 7:17

10

EXPLANATION AND EXAMPLES OF FAITH

As we turn to this section, we find ourselves in God's Hall of Fame. The exploits of the heroes of the faith are there before us. As we walk down the corridors, it is surprising to find that most of the heroes are laymen. As a matter of fact, only one clergyman is mentioned—Samuel—and then only in passing. Farmers, politicians, businessmen—these are the men God has singled out of the Old Testament for special recognition.

Dr. Howard G. Hendricks, well-known conference speaker, once stated, "There is no pleasing God without risk-taking." These men and women were willing to do just that. One thing they all had in common was their willingness to take great *risks* for God.

The object of our risk-taking determines what we call the risk we take. When the object of our risk-taking is horses, we call that gambling; when the object of our risk-taking is the stock market, we call that business; when the object of our risk-taking is God, we call that faith.

Risk-taking and faith, then, are synonyms, and the *object* of our faith determines its validity. Figure 25 on page 146 will help bring this into focus. In the first illustration (A), let us say that it is the dead of winter and the temperature is −20°F. There are about two feet of ice on the surface of the pond, and I have to cross over it. So I ask you, "Will the ice hold me?"

Figure 25

THE OBJECT OF OUR FAITH DETERMINES THE VALIDITY OF OUR FAITH
I DON'T HAVE TOO MUCH FAITH, BUT I'LL TRY IT!
FAITH
SAFE
THICK ICE
I KNOW I'LL MAKE IT--- I HAVE LOTS OF FAITH!
FAITH
DANGER
THIN ICE
A
B

"Most certainly," you assure me.

But I am not so sure about your assurance, and crawl across the pond with fear and trembling. Do I get across? Yes, easily.

In the second drawing (B), we change the circumstances and say that it is spring, and there is only a one-inch layer of ice on the pond. I again ask you if it will hold me, and you discourage me from trying. I accuse you of a lack of faith, and charge across, only to fall through into the cold water.

What lesson can we learn from this? In the first instance, we saw that strong ice and weak faith resulted in a safe crossing. In the second instance, weak ice and strong faith resulted in disaster. It was not the amount of faith but the thickness of the ice that made the difference. The object of your faith (in this case the ice), determines the validity of your faith.

In the Bible, this principle is also true. For this reason, the writer of Hebrews spends the better part of his letter talking about the object of our faith—Jesus Christ. Because He is none other than the Creator God, who became a man so that He could offer Himself as a sacrifice for our sins, He is better than any other object in which we can put our faith. Our faith does not save us. The object of our faith does.

When circumstances in life become hard to bear, we are exhorted to hold on to the object of our faith, even Jesus Christ. The circumstances facing those whom the writer was addressing were unbelievably difficult, and this is the advice that he offered them: "Endure, remembering who the object of your faith is."

Not only did the people in this section have great faith, almost all of them had difficult circumstances in their lives at some time or other. These saints are not mentioned for us because God helped them, for God promises to help anyone who calls on Him. They are here because when the going got rough, they did not abandon their commitment to God and begin to retreat.

Someone once said, "Circumstances don't break a man; they reveal him." Tried in the furnace of adversity, these people did not break. They were actually made stronger.

We can study this important chapter under three major headings (note Figure 24, page 144).

- Explanation of Faith (11:1-3)
- Examples of Faith (11:4-31)
- Exploits of Faith (11:32-40)

Though the first part provides us with a concise definition of faith, it is helpful to look first at the other two parts to see how faith works itself out in practice. Then we can return and view from hindsight how the writer of Hebrews crystalizes the concept of faith into a definition and explanation.

Examples of Faith

Our writer takes us back to the Book of Genesis to see his first examples. Then we join the children of Israel walking out of their captivity in Egypt and into the Promised Land, and in so doing, observe the heroes of the faith who led them.

The Patriarchs — Hebrews 11:4-22

> [4]By faith Abel offered God a better sacrifice than Cain did. By faith he was commended as a righteous man, when God spoke well of his offerings. And by faith he still speaks, even though he is dead.
>
> [5]By faith Enoch was taken from this life, so that he did not experience death; he could not be found, because God had taken him away. For before he was taken, he was commended as one who pleased God. [6]And without faith it is impossible to please God, because anyone who comes to him must believe that he exists and that he rewards those who earnestly seek him.
>
> [7]By faith Noah, when warned about things not yet seen, in holy fear built an ark to save his family. By his faith he condemned the world and became heir of the righteousness that comes by faith.
>
> [8]By faith Abraham, when called to go to a place he would later receive as his possession, obeyed and went, even though he did not know where he was going. [9]By faith he made his home in the promised land like a stranger in a foreign country; he lived in tents, as did Isaac and Jacob, who were heirs with him of the same promise. [10]For he was looking forward to the city with foundations, whose architect and builder is God.
>
> [11]By faith even Sarah, who was past age was enabled to bear children because she considered him faithful who had made the promise [margin]. [12]And so from this one man, and he as good as dead, came descendants as numerous as the stars in the sky and as countless as the sand of the seashore.
>
> [13]All these people were still living by faith when they died. They did not receive the things promised; they only saw them and welcomed them from a distance. And they admitted that they were foreigners and strangers on earth. [14]People who say such things show that they are looking for a country of their own.

[15]If they had been thinking of the country they had left, they would have had an opportunity to return. [16]Instead, they were longing for a better country—a heavenly one. Therefore God is not ashamed to be called their God, for he has prepared a city for them.

[17]By faith Abraham, when God tested him, offered Isaac as a sacrifice. He who had received the promises was about to sacrifice his one and only son, [18]even though God had said to him, "Through Isaac shall your promised offspring come." [19]Abraham reasoned that God could raise the dead, and figuratively speaking, he did receive Isaac back from death.

[20]By faith Isaac blessed Jacob and Esau in regard to their future.

[21]By faith Jacob, when he was dying, blessed each of Joseph's sons, and worshiped as he leaned on the top of his staff.

[22]By faith Joseph, when his end was near, spoke about the exodus of the Israelites from Egypt and gave instructions about his bones.

As I was studying Hebrews with a group of men, one of them pointed out that it is possible to see the life of faith worked out in the patriarchs in the following way:

Verse 4—"By faith Abel offered God a better sacrifice. In Abel's life, we find the *sacrifice* of faith.

Verse 5—Moses said, "Enoch walked with God, then he was no more, because God took him away" (Gen. 5:24). In Enoch, we see the *walk* of faith.

Verse 7—"By faith Noah . . . built an ark." In Noah, we note the *work* of faith.

Verse 8—"By faith Abraham, when called . . . , obeyed." In Abraham's life, we observe the *obedience* of faith.

Verse 11—"Through faith also Sarah herself received strength to conceive seed, and was delivered of a child when she was past age, because she judged Him faithful who had promised" (KJV). In Sarah's life, we see the *willingness* of faith.

Verses 13-16—"All these people were still living by faith when they died. . . . They admitted that they were foreigners and strangers on earth." In all their lives, we are confronted by the *anticipation* of faith.

The Exodus and the Conquest — Verses 23-31

[23]By faith Moses' parents hid him for three months after he

was born, because they saw he was no ordinary child, and they were not afraid of the king's edict.

[24]By faith Moses, when he had grown up, refused to be known as the son of Pharaoh's daughter. [25]He chose to be mistreated along with the people of God rather than to enjoy the pleasures of sin for a short time. [26]He regarded disgrace for the sake of Christ as of greater value than the treasures of Egypt, because he was looking ahead to his reward. [27]By faith he left Egypt, not fearing the king's anger; he persevered because he saw him who is invisible. [28]By faith he kept the Passover and the sprinkling of blood, so that the destroyer of the firstborn would not touch the firstborn of Israel.

[29]By faith the people passed through the Red Sea as on dry land; but when the Egyptians tried to do so, they were drowned.

[30]By faith the walls of Jericho fell, after the people had marched around them for seven days.

[31]By faith the prostitute Rahab, because she welcomed the spies, was not killed with those who were disobedient.

The story of Moses begins with his mother and father exercising faith. The Pharaoh of Egypt had decreed that Israel's male babies were to be destroyed. Believing that the commands of God took precedence over the commands of the king, these godly parents decided in faith to hide their infant boy.

Then it was *Moses* who exercised decisions by faith, the same kind of hard decisions his parents had made earlier (vv. 24-28). Raised in an environment of faith, he embraced it as his own in later years. The challenge and encouragement to those raising children is obvious.

When did his parents' faith become Moses' faith? The writer says, "When he had grown up." As a child Moses believed the same things his parents believed. Is this not true of most young children? If their parents believe in Jesus, generally so do they. If you ask my little daughter where Jesus lives, she will tell you, "In my heart."

There comes a day, however, when believing what the parents believe merely because they believe it, no longer is valid. When a person grows up, he must develop his own set of convictions. Moses believed the right things for the right reasons, and right actions followed. He had developed his own convictions. He *refused* identification with the Egyptian court (v. 24); he *chose* to suffer with the people of God (v. 25); he *forsook* Egypt (v. 27).

An unshakable faith must be built on unshakable convictions, and these must be the product of your own life experiences. *You* must meet God and get to know Him. No one else can do it for you. In the time of testing—and the time will come—no one else's convictions will do. They must be your own.

This is the first cornerstone in the life of faith. The second is found in these words: "[Moses] was looking ahead to his reward" (v. 26). J. B. Phillips puts it this way: "He looked steadily at the ultimate, not the immediate, reward." Moses had what might be called bifocal vision, which is the ability to see the immediate in the light of eternity. That's perspective!

Joe was an undergraduate university student when God first captured his heart with the vision of reaching the world for Christ. There was a cutting edge to his life as he measured every decision he made by this all-consuming goal. On graduation, he vowed to spend his life serving the Lord. Then came marriage, quickly followed by a young growing family. Now a family needs a home, and a home needs furnishings; the children need an education, and he and his wife will have to prepare for retirement.

Joe's son Bill is now a freshman in college and returns home during the holidays obsessed with the same vision of reaching the world for Christ that had captured his father years earlier. Every time his son is home, however, it is as though a knife pierces Joe's heart, for he can see in Bill's zeal how much his own love for the Savior has waned. What was the problem? How could it have happened? How could "things" have blunted his initial commitment to Christ so thoroughly? Joe had lost perspective. He had failed to maintain a bifocal vision.

Moses found his way into the annals of God's great men because, regardless of the circumstances, he never lost his perspective. The same was true with the Israelites (v. 29), Joshua (v. 30), and Rahab (v. 31).

Exploits of Faith

As we read through this passage, note carefully how God delivers His people *from* their difficulties. Enemy armies, evil men, wild animals—nothing could touch them. Miracles surrounded their lives.

Deliverance From Persecution—Hebrews 11:32-35a

> [32]And what more shall I say? I do not have time to tell about Gideon, Barak, Samson, Jephthah, David, Samuel and the prophets, [33]who by faith conquered kingdoms, administered justice, and gained what was promised; who shut the mouths of lions, [34]quenched the fury of the flames, and escaped the edge

of the sword; whose weakness was turned to strength; and who became powerful in battle and routed foreign armies. [35]Women received back their dead, raised to life again.

In the middle of verse 35 the story changes. Miracles cease and everything apparently goes wrong. Now people are badly treated and killed. Had God abandoned them? No; they wouldn't have made His Hall of Fame if He had. Let us read about this strange phenomenon.

Deliverance Through Persecution—Hebrews 11:35b-40

Others were tortured and refused to be released, so that they might gain a better resurrection. [36]Some faced jeers and flogging, while still others were chained and put in prison. [37]They were stoned; they were sawed in two; they were put to death by the sword. They went about in sheepskins and goatskins, destitute, persecuted and mistreated—[38]the world was not worthy of them. They wandered in deserts and mountains, and in caves and holes in the ground.

[39]These were all commended for their faith, yet none of them received what had been promised. [40]God had planned something better for us so that only together with us would they be made perfect.

Was the faith of those in the first group greater than that of the people mentioned in the second? Not at all. How then can we explain such a radical difference? By the *type* of faith by which God asked them to walk. To illustrate, we can call the first *Noah Faith* (vv. 32-35a), and the faith expressed in the second part *Job Faith* (vv. 35b-40). For God delivered Noah *from* the flood of adversity, but He delivered Job *through* the flood of adversity. Let's take a look at both.

Both Noah and Job were required to walk by faith. The risk for each was the same. The advantage that Noah had over Job was that he knew exactly what God was doing, why He was doing it, and how it was going to be done. Noah probably never had any doubt about God's plan and what he himself had to do to get ready for it. Job, however, knew nothing. He didn't know what God was doing or why He was doing it. If only Job could have overheard the conversations between God and Satan (Job 1–2), his sufferings might have been easier to bear. If only God had taken him into His confidence, . . . but such was not to be. Job was totally in the dark. Noah had to trust the *promise* of God; Job had to trust the *character* of God.

The advantage that Job had over Noah, however, was that he didn't have to do a thing. The success or failure of the mission wasn't dependent on any action Job needed to take. All that was required of him was to sit tight and weather the storm. Not so for Noah. Success or failure rested squarely with him. He had to cut down the trees, make the ship, and gather in all the animals and provisions.

God calls on us to walk by different types of faith at different times in our lives. The Lord may give us a promise and expect us to act on it. We are staggered by the implications, and it takes all the courage we can muster to step out by faith.

Then there are things that cross our path that have all the hallmarks of tragedy and disaster. God seems to be silent. No word from Him on what He is doing or why. No promise. Nothing. But His all-sufficient grace and comfort are there. If we were not confident of His love and sovereign control, we would conclude that He had abandoned us.

When God calls us to walk by faith—it matters not what type—our natural tendency is immediately to long for the other type. If Christ asks us to sell our home, quit our job, and go somewhere else by faith, we begin longing for the Job-type faith. If our loved one is involved in an auto accident, immediately we long for the Noah-type faith by asking God for some word as to why. The plain truth is that neither type of faith is pleasant. It is never easy to walk by faith.

When my wife and I first learned that our oldest boy had leukemia, I went out to the park and wept till there were no tears left in me. My son and I were extremely close and the thought of losing him was more than I felt my heart could bear. Some good friends owned a cabin out on a lake and I went there for three days of prayer and fasting to see if God had a word for me. Was there something in my life the Lord wanted removed that was of such a nature that *this* was required to get my attention?

I am as sinful a man as many and more sinful than most, but the Lord assured me that He was not punishing me for sin. Jesus had taken the punishment for me on the cross. "Why then, Lord?" I asked. "Why are You doing this? Give me a promise. Break the silence and speak to me."

But the Lord was silent. It was as though He had said, "No promise, Walt. My *character* is enough."

Our son slipped into the presence of Jesus several years ago, and to this day I don't know why God took him. It would be wonderful if I could say, "Because of his death *these* people came to Christ, or, it made a tremendous difference in *that* situation." But I can't. I can see no appreciable difference that resulted from his death, and probably never will this side of heaven. But God's character is sufficient.

In many respects, it requires more faith to be delivered through the difficulty (vv. 35b-40) than from the trouble (vv. 32-35a). It is important that we know that God has His Hand on us in either case. If this is not clear in our experience, then when adversity comes we will be tempted to conclude that God has forsaken us when such is simply not the case. We are being asked to walk by (Job) faith, and how we respond will determine if we make God's Hall of Fame.

Explanation of Faith — *Hebrews 11:1-3*

> [1]Now faith is being sure of what we hope for and certain of what we do not see. [2]This is what the ancients were commended for.
>
> [3]By faith we understand that the universe was formed at God's command, so that what is seen was not made out of what was visible.

Having looked at all but the first three verses of this great chapter, let us turn to them and examine them in the light of what we have already learned. We will study the *definition of faith* as it is illustrated in the bottom half of Figure 24 on page 144. This figure suggests that *faith is obeying the promises of God.* Obeying here has the idea of "acting on." When God commits Himself, revealing to us what He wants done and we act on it, this is faith. The three key words in this definition are *faith, promises,* and *obedience.* We will look at them in that order.

Faith

We can paraphrase the opening statement thus: "Now faith is being sure of what we hope for and certain of what we do not see" (v. 1). *What we hope for* is the future, and *what we do not see* is the invisible. So immediately we grasp the fact that faith can be demonstrated in only two areas: in the future and in the invisible.

An illustration may help clarify this. As a single man working with The Navigators, I fell in love with a beautiful brunette named Leette Dillon. She agreed to marry me about the same time the organization asked me to represent it with the Wycliffe Bible Translators at their pioneer missionary training camp in the jungles of Chiapas, Mexico. For several months I ministered in Mexico while Leette lived in the United States.

We corresponded frequently. In her letters, she promised me two things. Her first promise was: "When you return I will marry you." I would read those words over and over again. They were particularly important to me because I had to take them by faith; they had to do with the future. Now we have been married a number of years, and I don't take our marriage by faith; it is a present and past experience and does not require faith. As a matter of fact, I would consider it strange if Leette felt the need to say to me, "Sweetheart, we are married!"

The other "promise" contained in Leette's letters was: "I love you." This I also took by faith and can still clearly remember walking down many jungle trails rehearsing those words over and over again. It required faith to believe it, for love is "not seen." It is an intangible, invisible thing, and even though we have been married a number of years I still take Leette's love for me by faith.

This is the reason I never get bored with her telling me of her love, even though I don't have to be reminded that we are married. She can tell me she loves me in a thousand different ways *each day* and I would never grow tired of it. Because love must be taken by faith, it is imperative that our loved ones hear it from us often. Faith needs reinforcement. This is why we need to express it to others, and why we need to be diligent in our appropriation of the Scriptures so we can hear it from the Lord.

The writer states that faith is the "guarantee and proof" of what is future and invisible. From this we realize that it is only after one acts by faith, doing what God wants done, that one knows it works. The experience of faith is the very proof of faith. As Christians, we cannot prove to the skeptic that God exists, but we can introduce him to God. He, in exercising faith toward God, can realize for himself that God really does exist.

Faith is a dimension of reality that is valid only to the person who has walked by faith. Saying it another way, commitment comes before knowledge. "Commitment" has to do with *obedience* (we will talk further about this concept later). Only after Noah built the ship did he know whether God really would send the rain. It was only after Moses obeyed God and went down to confront Pharaoh that he knew God would work on his behalf with the plagues.

Faith builds faith. The person who trusts God for the little things in life finds his confidence in God growing in preparation for the big things. Abraham's previous walk of faith prepared him for his willingness to offer his son Isaac. This is one of the greatest expressions of faith in the Bible, for Abraham in obeying God's command to sacrifice Isaac was *disobeying* God's moral command not to kill, which was written in his conscience.

Put yourself in Abraham's sandals. Imagine yourself receiving such a command. Then visualize it coming to you in the most favorable way so as to draw maximum credence. Would you believe it came from God? "Take your son and kill him." If this command came written in the clouds, you would shrug it off as a quirk in nature. If an angel told you to do it, you would conclude that it was really Satan disguised as "an angel of light." In what form could God tell you to do such a thing and you would believe it to be from God? In all probability, in no way at all.

What then prompted Abraham to obey? What made him so sure it was God speaking to him? It was the result of a whole series of experiences Abraham had with God through the years, learning to trust God in the little things. He had become so accustomed to listening to God that he had no doubt it was God who had given him the command to climb Mount Moriah and sacrifice his son.

The only way to prepare yourself for the big crises in life is to learn to hear the voice of God in the day-by-day experiences of walking by faith. Each expression of faith builds confidence for the next.

Promises

Faith without the promises of God is no faith at all; it amounts to mere presumption. The promises of God are essential for the walk of faith. Let me illustrate with a hypothetical situation. We are flying together in a small aircraft, circling over your city at 15,000 feet. Feeling quite spiritual, I ask you, "If I jump from this plane, do you think God could catch me?"

You hesitate, so I respond to your silence by saying, "O you of little faith, let me show you." So I leap out without a parachute. On my way down, I suddenly realize to my horror that though God *can* catch me, He never *promised* me that He would. My expression of faith was not faith at all. It was presumption.

The difference between the Israelites and the Egyptians illustrates this point clearly: "By faith the people [Israelites] passed through the Red Sea as on dry land; but when the Egyptians tried to do so, they were drowned" (Heb. 11:29). The Red Sea was open for both of them. Both crossed by faith. The Israelites had a promise from God and crossed safely. The Egyptians did not; they crossed presumptuously and were drowned.

When Abraham took Isaac up Mount Moriah to offer him as a sacrifice, he went with a promise, "Through Isaac shall your promised offspring come" (v. 18). Not in Ishmael, not in one of the sons of Keturah, but in *Isaac* was his seed to be called. Abraham must have reviewed that promise again and again as he and Isaac walked to the place of sacrifice. So confident was Abraham of God's promise that he believed that when he offered Isaac, God would raise him from the dead (v. 19).

A person can do many things in life without biblical faith. Without leaning on God, he can pick his spouse, choose a vocation, and possibly even make a lot of money. But there is one thing he cannot do without faith; he cannot please God. "Without faith it is impossible to please God, because anyone who comes to him must believe that he exists and that he rewards those who earnestly seek him" (v. 6). A person must "believe that he is"—that He is who He says He is—and "that he rewards those who earnestly seek him"—that He will do what He says He will do.

What are some of the promises God has given you—for your spouse, your family, your own personal life? Remember, no promises, no faith. The Apostle Peter stated, "Through these he has given us his very great and precious promises, so that through them you may participate in the divine nature and escape the corruption in the world caused by evil desires" (2 Peter 1:4). The Bible is full of "very great and precious promises"—for you!

The Bible is not the only place from which you can learn God's will, but it is the most important place. All that God has said through the centuries in these sacred pages is for you to learn from and apply. "But the plans of the Lord stand firm forever, the purposes of his heart through *all generations*" (Ps. 33:11).

If the idea of claiming God's promises is new to you, ask the Lord to give you a promise as you spend time with Him in the Bible. Don't try to force or extract one for yourself. Wait quietly on the Lord, and when He speaks to you through the Word, accept the promise and pray over it. If the Lord gives you the assurance that it is from Him, claim it and act on it.

Obedience

A promise without obedience isn't faith either; it is unbelief. Whenever God commits Himself to us by asking us to act, our unwillingness to do what He says amounts to unbelief. This has already been vividly illustrated for us in the incident of Israel at Kadesh Barnea (Heb. 3–4). God made His people a promise, but they refused to act on it. Instead, they became afraid of the giants, and God called it unbelief (Heb. 3:19). It took them forty years to recover from that tragic mistake.

Faith is always active; it is an exercise of the will. Note some of the action verbs in this chapter:

- *Verse 4*—By faith Abel *offered*
- *Verse 7*—By faith Noah *built*
- *Verse 8*—By faith Abraham *obeyed and went*
- *Verse 22*—By faith Joseph *gave instructions*
- *Verse 24*—By faith Moses *refused*

Earlier, we said that "commitment comes before knowledge" (p. 155). We *know* God will do what He promised only after we *obey*. Jesus said it succinctly, "If a man chooses to do God's will, he will find out whether my teaching comes from God or whether I speak on my own" (John 7:17). If we will do, then we will know. This concept is not unique to the Christian faith; it is required of every person in the general course of life.

Let us say that you are a heart surgeon and I come to you displaying some telltale symptoms of heart trouble, such as numbness in my arm. On examining me, you find I have a faulty valve in my heart and tell me that I will require open-heart surgery. You explain the process involved—opening my chest, stopping my heart, running my blood through a machine, repairing my heart, and sewing me up again. Apprehensively I ask if the operation will be successful. You try to encourage me with medical facts, and even introduce me to some of your patients who have undergone similar operations. My response is, "Fine, doctor, these are your successes. Now introduce me to your failures. Can you *guarantee* that the operation will be a success?" You, of course, cannot guarantee anything, so you simply suggest, "Climb up on the table and let me operate on you. When you wake up—*if* you wake up—you will know the operation was a success."

This is commitment before knowledge. This is faith. In this illustration, the object of my faith is the doctor. My willingness (or lack of it) to undergo the operation depends on how desperate I am. Suppose I say to you, "I don't want to know that badly," and you answer, "That's all right, but in six months you will be a dead man." On hearing that, I become desperate enough to undergo the operation.

Your willingness to take risks for God and act on what He has promised is related to your view of the options before you. The committed Christian has learned that if it is hard to walk by faith with God it is harder not to. It has always been hard to walk by faith, and it always will be.

Visualize Noah trying to do what God said. A huge ship is to be built on dry land with the nearest water miles away. Can you imagine him trying to explain it to his neighbors? They must have called it "Noah's Folly." Noah's greatest opposition probably came from his church. You can almost hear the elders talking things over with him. "This project of yours has the whole congregation in an uproar, Noah. If God wanted such a large ship built, don't you think He would have asked the whole church to do it? It is embarrassing for us having to explain your crazy project to the rest of the community. What we would like, Noah, is for you to get off this kick."

Or consider Abraham. God told him to pack up and leave home, "even though he did not know where he was going" (v. 8). How do you go about explaining that to your friends and neighbors? They might say, "You say that God spoke to you. And He wants you to leave. But you don't know where you are going. Are you sure you are feeling all right, Abraham?"

Or think about Moses. His life can be divided into three 40-year segments. The first 40 years were spent in the royal court—not a bad start. The next 40 years were spent in the desert taking care of another man's sheep. About two to three years were spent delivering Israel from Egypt. Then came the Kadesh Barnea crisis, and the last 40 years were spent burying his generation in the Sinai desert. Out of a life spanning 120 years, only two to three of them would be considered successful by the critical observer. The life of faith is not an easy life.

But it is rewarding. It is a life by which true greatness may be measured. Everyone has heard of Moses the great law-giver. Every Jew, Muslim, and Christian knows about and reveres him. Every educated person has heard of him. Not only does Moses live with God, but his memory continues to live with us. Faith is the key to the life of significance.

In conclusion, let's meditate on a passage in which we see the four-stage rocket to faith: "All these people were still living by faith when they died. They did not receive the things promised; they only *saw* them, were *persuaded* of them, and *welcomed* them from a distance. And they *admitted* that they were foreigners and strangers on earth'' (Heb. 11:13).

Now contrast this with Achan's confession of stealing after the battle of Jericho. ``When I *saw* in the plunder a beautiful robe from Babylon, two hundred shekels of silver and a wedge of gold weighing fifty shekels, I *coveted* them and *took* them. They are *hidden* in the ground inside my tent, with the silver underneath'' (Josh. 7:21). This is the four-stage rocket to sin.

The first stage for both cases starts with the eyes. After that they differ. Sin ends in hiding. It is the story of the Garden of Eden all over again—they saw, coveted, took, and hid. In contrast, faith ends in proclaiming the good news to all—saw, were persuaded, welcomed, and admitted.

The writer says of these people ``If they had been thinking of the country they had left, they would have had opportunity to return'' (Heb. 11:15). Why was it that they never turned back? Because it never crossed their minds. This is the single-minded commitment to faith.

``Instead, they were longing for a better country—a heavenly one. Therefore God is not ashamed to be called their God, for He has prepared a city for them'' (Heb. 11:16). This is one of the most remarkable statements in the Bible: ``God is not ashamed to be called their God.''

It is one thing for you to be known in reference to God as a child of God and a Christian. It is an entirely different matter for God to be known in reference to you. When men inquired into who God was, He said, ``I am the God of Abraham, Isaac, and Jacob.'' God revealed Himself as *their* God. This is one of the most amazing concepts in the Bible: that the Creator God would be known by reference to His creatures.

``God is not ashamed to be called their God.'' This is true for those who walk by faith.

HEBREWS 12:1–29

THE ENCUMBRANCES OF FAITH
Hebrews 12

Figure 26

FAITH				
Race of the Christian	Reason for Discipline	Response of the Disciplined	Relationship of Grace	Regard for the Word
12:1, 2	12:3-11	12:12-17	12:18-24	12:25-29
Example of Faith	Necessity of Faith	Failure of Faith	Approach of Faith	Response of Faith
Provision for Grace	Expression of Grace	Failing Grace	Access of Grace	Service of Grace
				WARNING

11

ENCUMBRANCES OF FAITH

Dick has the kind of job that brings a great deal of personal satisfaction to him. He is a physician specializing in internal diseases, and is highly regarded as a doctor. The only new patients he can take are those referred to him by other specialists.

Dick and I have enjoyed many long conversations about his practice and about some of the patients for whom he is responsible. His practice is vital to many. Their needs are great and the stakes involved are high. Most of his patients are suffering from debilitating diseases such as diabetes, tuberculosis, ulcers, cancer, and heart disease. Without the right sort of treatment given at the right time, many of these patients would spend the rest of their lives encumbered by diseases that would drastically reduce their effectiveness and limit their ability to function normally.

A person's spiritual life, similarly, is susceptible to a number of serious spiritual diseases. The Bible teaches that sin is the cause of *all* of man's problems. Guilt, anxiety, sickness, death, decay, and uncertainty are all products of sin. Many of the physical ailments people see their doctors about are often the symptoms of inner struggles and tensions.

A few of these spiritual diseases are identified for us in this section (Heb. 12). If not dealt with, they can cripple a person's effectiveness. The life of faith in the normal, spiritually healthy person is a life freed from these encumbrances.

The writer discusses five major problems that must be overcome. These may be divided into the parts shown in Figure 26 on page 162.

- Race of the Christian (12:1,2)
- Reason for Chastening (12:3-11)
- Response of the Chastened (12:12-17)
- Relationship of Grace (12:18-24)
- Regard for the Word (12:25-29)

Each part diagnoses one problem and gives the remedy for it.

Till now, we've been using the metaphor of health and sickness to describe the state of the believer in his life of faith. In the first part, the writer picks a different metaphor and describes the life of a Christian in terms of an athlete running a race in a vast, crowded arena (vv. 1-2). Shifting to this metaphor, we can view this section as presenting us with five hurdles the believer must leap over if he is to complete the "race of faith" successfully.

Race of the Christian — *Hebrews 12:1, 2*

> [1]Therefore, since we are surrounded by such a great cloud of witnesses, let us throw off everything that hinders and the sin that so easily entangles, and let us run with perseverance the race marked out for us. [2]Let us fix our eyes on Jesus, the author and perfecter of our faith, who for the joy set before him endured the cross, scorning its shame, and sat down at the right hand of the throne of God.

The writer concluded the previous section with this observation about the heroes of the faith: "These were all commended for their faith, yet none of them received what had been promised. God had planned something better for us so that only together with us would they be made perfect" (Heb. 11:39-40).

They did not receive "what had been promised." Earlier, he had said they "saw them . . . from a distance" (Heb. 11:13). One of the reasons these saints became great in the sight of God was that they staked their all on promises God would not be fulfilling in their lifetimes. Many of the promises were to find their fulfillment in the period of history in which *we* live.

Having run their race in the arena of life, they then filed into the stands to take their seats as spectators of the races that were to follow. In a very real sense, they have a stake in your performance, and you can sense the excitement in their voices as they encourage you on.

Your coach and pacesetter is Jesus Christ. He too ran the race of faith, performing as no other before or since. Now He is with you to encourage you over the hurdles along the track. He is with you, and not in the stands with the spectators. He is by your side.

The first hurdle that we must jump—the first disease that needs attention lest it cripple us—is found in this exhortation: "Let us lay aside *every weight*" (v. 1 KJV). The weight of "things" is the excess baggage that we accumulate in our journey through life. The more we possess the more we want. The luxuries of yesterday become the necessities of today. What used to be our possessions now possess us.

No one intends this to happen to him. It is just that ever so subtly we begin to depend on "things" more and more, till we feel we cannot do without them. Dependence is shifted from Jesus Christ to possessions.

Things in and of themselves are not evil. Many of the gold-medal winners in the Old Testament were wealthy men. The secret is in not being dependent on things, not feeling we *need* them and so making our decisions on the basis of these things. The persecuted Christians to whom the writer originally penned these words were able to accept "joyfully . . . the confiscation of [their] property" (Heb. 10:34). Their "things" were just not that important to them.

How then do we cure the disease of being weighed down by possessions? How do we leap this hurdle? By fixing "our eyes on Jesus, the author and perfecter of our faith." Christ is the *author* of our faith—He brought us into the life of faith. And He is the *perfecter*—we will never be able to win without Him.

The beautiful thing is that He *wants* us to win. In fact, He will go to great lengths to help free us of the *weights* that encumber us. It is precisely here that we need to exercise "perseverance" (v. 1). The Lord can help free us from our "weights" in many ways—through fire, breakage, theft, and loss.

We need to persevere because the Savior deals with us as His beloved children. This is the subject of the next paragraph.

Reason for Discipline — *Hebrews 12:3-11*

[3]Consider him who endured such opposition from sinful men, so that you will not grow weary and lose heart.

[4]In your struggle against sin, you have not yet resisted to the point of shedding your blood. [5]And you have forgotten that word of encouragement that addresses you as sons:

"My son, do not make light of the Lord's discipline,
and do not lose heart when he rebukes you,

> [6]because the Lord disciplines those whom he loves,
> and he punishes everyone he accepts as a son."
>
> [7]Endure hardship as discipline; God is treating you as sons. For what son is not disciplined by his father? [8]If you are not disciplined (and everyone undergoes discipline), then you are illegitimate children and not true sons. [9]Moreover, we have all had human fathers who disciplined us and we respected them for it. How much more should we submit to the Father of our spirits and live! [10]Our fathers disciplined us for a little while as they thought best; but God disciplines us for our good, that we may share in his holiness. [11]No discipline seems pleasant at the time, but painful. Later on, however, it produces a harvest of righteousness and peace for those who have been trained by it.

When the writer says, "No discipline seems pleasant at the time, but painful," all of us can identify with him. No one enjoys the heavy hand of rebuke.

On one occasion, I was about to spank my young daughter for doing wrong when she asked, "Dad, who spanks you when you do wrong?"

Somewhat taken aback by her question, I paused and, as calmly as possible, answered, "Those who watch over my soul and God are the ones who spank me."

Not satisfied with so glib an answer, she persisted, "How does God spank you?"

How *does* God spank the believer? That He does is evident from the passage, but *how* He does differs from person to person. Note some of the ways He deals with us.

God allows us to taste the fruit of our sins. Drunkenness is not the only sin that leaves a hang-over. Investing our money when we are prompted by greedy motives and without asking the Lord's counsel can easily result in loss rather than gain.

God allows us to get caught in our sins. My wife and I have told our children that we are asking the Lord not to let them get away with sins that other people seem to commit undetected.

God insists that we return to the point of departure before going any farther. We sometimes go off on a tangent in our Christian life and wander in the wilderness of sin and rebellion for a while. When we repent and return to the walk of faith, we don't return to where we would have been had we not sinned. Rather, we return to where we were before we got off the track.

God does not use us the way we could have been used. To me, this is one of the most severe and frightening forms of correction. Paul talks about it as a source of personal motivation in his letter to the Corinthians. "No, I beat my body and make it my slave so that after I have preached to others, I myself will not be disqualified for the prize" (1 Cor. 9:27). He's using the same metaphor as the writer does here—the race. He is afraid of Jesus the coach saying to him, "Step off the track; you are disqualified!"

The Lord can get our attention whenever He wants. There is no doubt about that. And He has never been short of ideas on how to do it. Why then does He discipline us? Because of His love for us (Heb. 12:6). It is only the illegitimate child for whom the father has no love who goes without correction (v. 8). God deals with us as a father deals with his beloved son. For the rhetorical question, "For what son is not disciplined by his father?" the answer is, "No one!" (v. 7)

A distinction must be maintained between *correction* and *punishment*. The chastening of the Lord in the life of the Christian is never punitive; it is always corrective. The penalty for our sins has already been paid by Jesus Christ. *Christ is the perfect High Priest.* His chastening in our lives is always corrective—to help us become the kind of people we ought to be.

As parents, we need to follow the example of Jesus Christ our pacesetter. We should not *punish* our children for their wrongdoing, but *correct* them. Jesus has paid the penalty for their sins, just as He has paid it for ours. Parental discipline is always for the purpose of correction—to help them become better children.

The writer then clarifies the difference between the Lord's correction and that of parents (v. 10). Parents correct as seems best to them, not always consistently and with the right motives. They are unable to view things from an altogether accurate and objective perspective. Our heavenly Father, however, is always accurate, consistent, and has our best interests at heart.

The hurdle to be jumped here is *ignorance*. The believer must understand that the discipline that comes into his life is sent to purge him and make him a better person. Surgery is never pleasant. It is a painful experience to have the Lord cut undesirable things from our lives.

The solution to the potentially crippling disease of ignorance is found in the statement that "later on, however, it produces a harvest of righteousness and peace for those who have been trained by it" (v. 11).

Failure to come to grips with the *reason for discipline* will lead to a spirit of bitterness. This is the subject of the next section.

Response of the Disciplined — *Hebrews 12:12-17*

[12]Therefore, strengthen your feeble arms and weak knees. [13]Make level paths for your feet, so that the lame may not be disabled, but rather healed.

[14]Make every effort to live in peace with all men and to be holy; without holiness no one will see the Lord. [15]See to it that no one misses the grace of God and that no bitter root grows up to cause trouble and defile many. [16]See that no one is sexually immoral, or is godless like Esau, who for a single meal sold his inheritance rights as the oldest son. [17]Afterward, as you know, when he wanted to inherit this blessing, he was rejected. He could bring about no change of mind, though he sought the blessing with tears.

No disease in the Christian life is so widespread and so debilitating as bitterness. One of the reasons for this is our unwillingness to identify it for what it is. The sickness is hidden under so many euphemistic terms. "I am not really bitter; I am just *hurt* over what they did," is an often-heard comment that illustrates this. We call it "righteous indignation," "a wounded spirit," "feelings of resentment," "self-pity," and a feeling of "not being wanted." There may be shades of difference between these statements, but how easily they can spill over into bitterness.

The problem is identified for us—a "bitter root" (v. 15). In the margin of my Bible next to this verse I have written, "Bitterness results from a real or a supposed ill treatment." It does not matter whether some one has *in fact* wronged you or you just imagine it to be so. The devastating effect is the same. The injustice done so plagues the mind that the inner person becomes wasted and consumed. He is so sensitive to the issue that the slightest reference or reminder instinctively triggers an immediate replay of the whole episode.

The tragedy is compounded by the fact that not only is the bitter person himself damaged, but the cancer spreads into the lives of others "to cause trouble and defile many." Bitterness is not a private sin. By its very nature, it constantly demands a hearing, seeking out those with sympathetic ears who should know how wretched and unfair a blow it was. Others are drawn in and forced to take sides, and discord is sown among the brethren.

The writer illustrates this with what happened to Isaac's oldest son,

Esau. Because he was the eldest, the birthright was legally his. For Esau, this meant that he would become heir to the messianic promises given to Abraham and Isaac. Yet the very fact that he was willing to sell the birthright to his younger brother at a moment of hunger shows that it and the promise meant little to him.

Jacob, whose name means "supplanter," is often viewed as the culprit and Esau as the cheated victim. Jacob also is regarded as a sissy—more interested in hanging around his mother than pursuing manly interests. Esau is seen as the man's man—the hunter—a man who loved the outdoors.

Whatever bad characteristics Jacob had, he considered the promise of God to his ancestor important and was willing to pay any price to obtain it. For this he was later called Israel, a "Prince with God."

Whatever good characteristics may be evident in the life of Esau, he obviously did not regard the birthright as something precious and irreplaceable, and was willing to sell it in exchange for a full stomach. For this he lost his place in history. Like so many other things in life, the inheritance, once lost, could never be regained. He would have to settle for second best forever.

In summarizing this passage, we see the three distinctive effects of a root of bitterness. The writer warns:

- "See to it that no one misses the grace of God" (v. 15). Though God's grace is readily available to him, his bitterness precludes his ability to appropriate it.
- "To cause trouble and defile many" (v. 15). Just as healthy cells in the body can be destroyed by neighboring malignant cells, so other people are damaged by the bitter person in their midst.
- "See that no one . . . godless like Esau" (v. 16). Once drawn into the net of bitterness, for some there is no way to repair the loss. What happened to Esau exemplifies the irrevocable consequences of a decision once made. A steady flow of tears is an appropriate expression of regret, but it cannot right the wrong. The damage has been done. Just as you cannot put toothpaste back into a tube, so there is no way to repair the damage done as the fruit of bitterness spreads.

Where, then, are we to look for the solution? What is the cure? We find it in the admonition that follows (v. 12-14). The "feeble arms" and "weak knees" mentioned here are references not to the physical, but to the spiritual anatomy.

The mind becomes frozen and paralyzed by *bitterness,* and it requires an act of the will to set it free. So the "level paths for your feet" is a reference to the need for the person trapped in bitterness to direct his thoughts toward a true and correct course that will lead to a right perspective. Failure to recognize that every circumstance that enters our lives is an expression of God's grace can so easily lead to bitterness.

As Christians we need constantly to remind ourselves that two and only two persons can hurt us—God and ourselves. No one else can touch us—including the devil—except by divine permission. Since God has our best interests at heart, the options are narrow. Only *you* can wreck your life! This means that the ill treatment that comes to you from the hand of another comes only by God's permission. In the final analysis, when you get bitter at someone, your battle is not really with him but with God who let that person "get you."

This does not, of course, absolve evil people of their guilt. The Bible assures us that the Lord holds such people responsible for the evil they do. But their evil intent *cannot* shape our destiny. That is God's prerogative.

This is an important issue, and a biblical example may help clarify it. King David murdered Uriah the Hittite in order to cover up his adultery with Bathsheba (see 2 Sam. 11). When Uriah arrived in heaven, do you suppose God said, "Uriah, what are you doing here? Oh, I wish David had not caused you to die. I had such wonderful plans for you." No, more likely God said, "Enter, Uriah, I was expecting you. I shaped your destiny, and you are here by My perfect will in accordance with My perfect timetable." Having said this, however, God held David directly responsible for his sin (see 2 Sam. 12).

So the writer to the Hebrews says, "Make every effort to live in peace with all men" (v. 14). When bitterness begins to creep into your life, the only cure is to maintain a proper perspective. Remember that the sovereign God is in control and your problem is not with that other person. Go and follow the path of peace with him. Put your heart at ease. To the degree that he is at fault, God will deal with him. The unkind word or deed only touched your life because God allowed it.

God has your best interest at heart, and this must be accepted by faith. It is not, however, groundless faith. The writer has already carefully laid the foundation that leads you to conclude that God really does love you (see Heb. 1:1–10:18). The application of that love must be in the form of commitment—the kind of commitment called for in the rest of the book.

When adversity strikes in the form of persecution, the death of a loved one, financial disaster, or any number of other possible ways, it becomes all too easy to question God's goodness and God's love. Flirting with such thoughts can only lead to bitterness. "How could a loving God allow this to happen to me?" is a question we want to ask. When tempted with such thoughts, we need perspective. We leap the hurdle of bitterness by reminding ourselves of who God is and the irrevocable commitment He has made to us.

Relationship of Grace — *Hebrews 12:18-24*

> [18]You have not come to a mountain that can be touched and that is burning with fire; to darkness, gloom and storm; [19]to a trumpet blast or to such a voice speaking words, so that those who heard it begged that no further word be spoken to them, [20]because they could not bear what was commanded: "If even an animal touches the mountain, it must be stoned." [21]The sight was so terrifying that Moses said, "I am trembling with fear."
>
> [22]But you have come to Mount Zion, to the heavenly Jerusalem, the city of the living God. You have come to thousands upon thousands of angels in joyful assembly, [23]to the church of the firstborn, whose names are written in heaven. You have come to God, the judge of all men, to the spirits of righteous men made perfect, [24]to Jesus the mediator of a new covenant, and to the sprinkled blood that speaks a better word than the blood of Abel.

This passage contrasts Mount Sinai with Mount Zion. The first speaks of law, the second of grace. Law did not precede grace; quite the contrary. Grace was the foundation of the Abrahamic Covenant, and as Paul says, the law, which was introduced at Mount Sinai 430 years after Abraham, cannot disannul the Abrahamic Covenant of Grace (see Gal. 3:17). The fulfillment of this gracious covenant came with Jesus Christ.

Though grace was not a new concept to the Old Testament people of God, who even boasted, "We have Abraham to our father," nonetheless they chose to look to Mount Sinai. The allegory of Isaac and Ishmael makes this point (see Gal. 4:22-31). Rather than cling to Abraham and Mount Zion, the Jews of the writer's day clung to Moses and Mount Sinai.

This was indeed a tragic error for the Hebrew Christians to whom this letter was written. The writer urges these Jews again and again not to repeat this mistake during their time of testing.

The law of Sinai produced a fear relationship (see Heb. 12:18-21). The terror of the law was such that the people urged Moses to ask God not to speak to them in this way again (see Deut. 5:24-27). Even Moses regarded it as a *fearful* experience.

Fear enters our relationship with God when we view it as being the result of what we do. If our acceptance by God is dependent on our performance, as was the case with the Mosaic covenant, we have cause to fear. Read this covenant and note the conditions specified.

> "Now if you obey me fully and keep my covenant, then out of all nations you will be my treasured possession. Although the whole earth is mine, you will be for me a kingdom of priest and a holy nation." These are the words you are to speak to the Israelites."
>
> So Moses went back and summoned the elders of the people and set before them all the words the Lord had commanded him to speak. The people all responded together. "We will do everything the Lord has said." So Moses brought their answer back to the Lord. . . .
>
> The Lord descended to the top of Mount Sinai and called Moses to the top of the mountain. So Moses went up and the Lord said to him, "Go down and warn the people so they do not force their way through to see the Lord and many of them perish" (Exod. 19:5-8,20-21).

Fear, like bitterness, is a crippling disease. It can paralyze a person into inactivity. When a relationship is viewed as based on performance rather than on love and acceptance, fear is the natural outcome. How important it is to jump this hurdle in the life of faith.

The cure is easy to see. It is spelled out for us in the admonition to look to Mount Zion, not Sinai, to Jesus and Abraham, not Moses. The Mosaic covenant of law did not replace the Abrahamic covenant of grace. The law was given to teach us our need for Christ. It was never intended to be the basis of our relationship with God.

Every relationship must by its very nature be conditional, except our relationship with God. My closest earthly relationship is with my wife, yet I know that if I did certain things, I would force her to leave me, and vice versa. Our relationships with one another must be conditional simply because we are unable to predict behavior. It is still possible for Leette and me to surprise one another even after many years of marriage.

With God, however, it is a different matter altogether. Nothing we have ever done or will ever do will come as a surprise to Him. He is all-knowing. His gracious commitment to us is, for this reason, unconditional. He knows us as we will always be and He has accepted us as we are. We may disappoint the Lord, but we will never surprise Him.

Fear need not encumber us in the race. Let us leap this hurdle and move on in the Christian life!

Regard for the Word — *Hebrews 12:25-29*

> [25]See to it that you do not refuse him who speaks. If they did not escape when they refused him who warned them on earth, how much less will we, if we turn away from him who warns us from heaven? [26]At that time his voice shook the earth, but now he has promised, "Once more I will shake not only the earth but also the heavens." [27]The words "once more" indicate the removing of what can be shaken—that is, created things—so that what cannot be shaken may remain.
>
> [28]Therefore, since we are receiving a kingdom that cannot be shaken, let us be thankful, and so worship God acceptably with reverence and awe, [29]for our God is a consuming fire.

Here we have the fifth warning of the book (see Figure 1 on page 8). This warning is basically a repetition of the first one. The writer began by exhorting his audience to "heed the Word," and here he ends on the same note.

To make his point, the writer refers to what he wrote earlier. God's voice had been heard from Mount Sinai (see vv. 18-21). It was a terrifying experience. Now he says that God's voice "shook the earth." It is folly to suppose that because we have entered into a gracious relationship with the Lord it is no longer necessary to heed His Word.

Peter tells us, "The day of the Lord will come like a thief. The heavens will disappear with a roar; the elements will be destroyed by fire, and the earth and everything in it will be laid bare" (2 Peter 3:10). God is not through shaking the earth. And next time it won't be just the earth, "but also the heavens" (Heb. 12:26). This is when God will consummate human history in His Son Jesus Christ.

The writer is warning his audience of the temptation of *disobedience*. This hurdle looms on the horizon as soon as we begin thinking that grace permits licence, "God has irrevocably committed Himself to me, so now I can do whatever I want." This kind of thinking is a one-way road to disaster.

Never allow yourself to forget that there is a profound difference between the forgiveness of God and the consequences of sin. We have already mentioned David's sin of adultery with Bathsheba and the murder of her husband, Uriah. God forgave David, but the consequences of his sin lingered with him the rest of his life.

Overcome by depression or grief, you may leap from a tall building, intent on suicide. On the way down, you may realize your folly and cry to God for help and forgiveness. He will forgive you and restore fellowship, but He will probably not stop the fall.

The cure for the disease of *disobedience* is somewhat paradoxical. We are told to "fear" (vv. 28-29, KJV). Now fear was the hurdle we had just cleared; are we being told to return to it here? The word is the same, but the application, however, is entirely different. The fear mentioned here (v. 28) is not the fear of not being accepted by God, but rather the fear of the awful consequences of sin. It is a "godly fear," "reverence and awe." It means we are willing to appropriate the grace of God, "and so worship God acceptably."

In discussing this chapter, we have mixed the metaphors of medicine and field events in the hope of clarifying the great truths contained in this passage. The exhortation is for us to be free from the encumbrances that affect the Christian life, free from those sins that impede growth and fruitfulness. The solution to each encumbrance is found in a dimension of life defined by the writer as faith. "Look beyond the circumstance to the God who controls the circumstances and rest your case there."

As we press on through life, running round the track of the daily grind, let us keep fixing our "eyes on Jesus, the author and perfecter of our faith."

HEBREWS 13:1–25

Figure 27

EXPRESSIONS OF FAITH
Hebrews 13

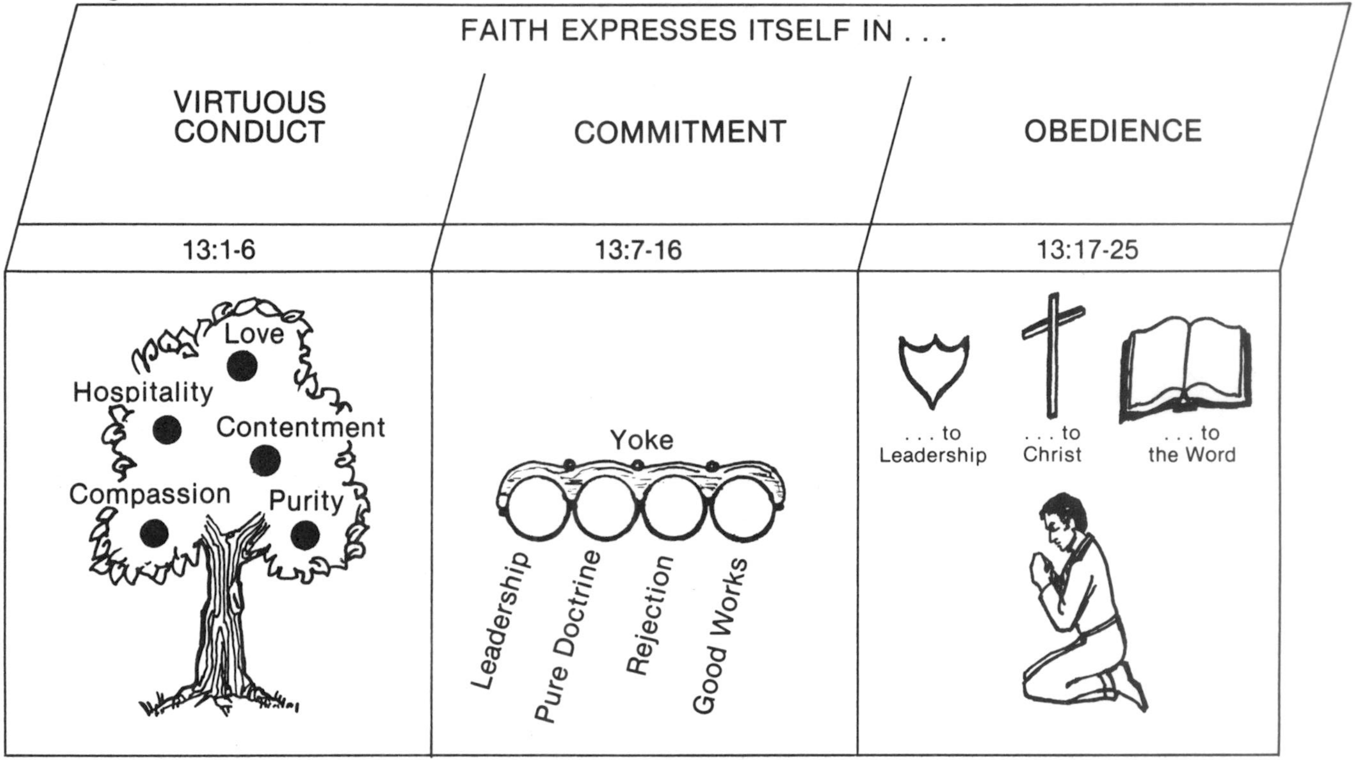

FAITH EXPRESSES ITSELF IN . . .

VIRTUOUS CONDUCT	COMMITMENT	OBEDIENCE
13:1-6	13:7-16	13:17-25
Love, Hospitality, Contentment, Compassion, Purity	Yoke: Leadership, Pure Doctrine, Rejection, Good Works	. . . to Leadership; . . . to Christ; . . . to the Word

12

EXPRESSIONS OF FAITH

For twelve magnificent chapters, the writer of the Epistle to the Hebrews has allowed us to drink deeply at his well, and what an experience it has been! Jesus Christ has been the topic of the conversation as He has been contrasted, compared, evaluated, and studied against the backdrop of the Old Testament.

The heart of man's problem has been revealed. Sin blocks man's access to God. It is a universal problem intrinsic in all the religions of the world. Man futilely builds his ladders to God, hoping that his efforts will appease God's wrath and somehow gain him entrance into heaven. Sacrifices are offered and rituals performed, but how is the conscience to be cleansed? How can guilt be forgiven?

Certainly not by self effort. Given a million years, man still could not atone for his own sins. A holy, righteous God cannot be in fellowship with sinful man any more than light can coexist with darkness. A God who winks at sin, under the pretext of love, has forfeited those very qualities that set Him apart as God.

How then can a holy and just God express His love? Only by paying the penalty of sin Himself, and this He did in the person of Jesus Christ. This is the reason Jesus could talk about love the way He did. He knew how much it cost.

Using the tabernacle worship as an illustration, the writer revealed Jesus as our High Priest, Sacrifice, and Holy of Holies. Through

Him, access to God is assured. Through Him, the justice of God is satisfied, our consciences are purged, and we are reconciled to God. Through Him, we see the love of God perfectly revealed.

The writer then presented us with the example of men who in former times had had their lives touched with this love, and he admonished us to follow their example. In light of God's love for us, the only reasonable response we can make is to live the life of faith wholeheartedly. Isaac Watts grasped this idea when he wrote:

When I survey the wondrous cross
on which the Prince of glory died,
My richest gain I count but loss
And pour contempt on all my pride.

Forbid it, Lord, that I should boast
Save in the death of Christ my God;
All the vain things that charm me most
I sacrifice them to His blood.

See, from His head, His hands, His feet,
Sorrow and love flow mingled down;
Did e'er such love and sorrow meet
Or thorns compose so rich a crown?

Were the whole realm of nature mine,
That were a present far too small:
Love so amazing, so divine,
Demands my soul, my life, my all.

How can a faith like this find its proper expression? The answer brings a fitting close to the subject of the greatness of Jesus Christ. We will study the writer's reply in three parts given in Figure 27 on page 176.

- Faith Expresses Itself in Virtuous Conduct (13:1-6)
- Faith Expresses Itself in Commitment (13:7-16)
- Faith Expresses Itself in Obedience (13:17-25)

Certain characteristics can be considered essential for the Christian life. In the first part, five of these are listed for us. We can call them the basics of Christian behavior.

Faith Expresses Itself in Virtuous Conduct — *Hebrews 13:1-6*

[1]Keep on loving each other as brothers. [2]Do not forget to entertain strangers, for by so doing some people have entertained angels without knowing it. [3]Remember those in prison as if you were their fellow prisoners, and those who are mistreated as if you yourselves were suffering.

[4]Marriage should be honored by all, and the marriage bed kept pure, for God will judge the adulterer and all the sexually immoral. [5]Keep your lives free from the love of money and be content with what you have, because God has said,

"Never will I leave you;
never will I forsake you."

[6]So we say with confidence,

"The Lord is my helper;
I will not be afraid.
What can man do to me?"

These qualities of virtuous conduct are to be sought after diligently. It is hard enough to apply these admonitions when conditions are most favorable. For these saints undergoing severe pressure daily, it was extremely hard. Now if they were expected to comply, how much more should we, who know so little of persecution and opposition. The five qualities are love, hospitality, compassion, purity, and contentment.

Love — v. 1

Jesus said, "All men will know that you are my disciples if you love one another" (John 13:35). This is a theme constantly repeated throughout the New Testament.

During the 1920s and 1930s, when fundamental Christianity was in the minority and fighting for its very survival, a sharp line was drawn between those who were "faithful" to the Bible and those who had "capitulated." Any form of compromise by the latter was treated in a harsh and censorious way by the former.

It is particularly during any severe time of testing that there is a tendency to see heresy in every form of disagreement. But there is a delicate balance between insisting on pure doctrine and showing "brotherly love." The writer to the Hebrews has certainly given a beautiful example of how it is to be done as he himself, in love, exhorts the brothers to hold fast to the faith. There can never be any excuse not to love.

Hospitality — v. 2

Prior to the destruction of Sodom and Gomorrah, God sent two angels to rescue Lot and his family from impending doom They spent the night with Lot, and Lot's receiving of them is an example of showing hospitality to angels who are not recognized as such by their host. (Gen. 19:1-3). Our writer is not suggesting that we should entertain strangers in the hopes of an angelic visit, but rather, that by opening our homes to strangers we may be blessed as were those in the Old Testament who were visited by angels.

Near the middle of the first century, at the time this letter was written, Christians were fleeing for their lives across the Roman Empire. Fellow believers opened their homes to these fugitives and in so doing jeopardized their own safety. Such hospitality is an essential part of the Christian faith.

The proliferation of restaurants and hotels today has all but made this a thing of the past. When, for example, was the last time you purposely laid an extra place for Sunday dinner in the event of meeting a stranger at the morning worship service in your church? When I attended seminary in a little community on the eastern shore of Lake Michigan, all the restaurants were closed on Sunday. How I appreciated being invited to a home for a meal. If no invitations were forthcoming, I was forced to fast.

Compassion — v. 3

Not all the Christian fugitives found shelter and safety in the homes of fellow believers. Many, some of whom were known to the writer's audience, had been caught and imprisoned for their faith. Though the writer does not suggest how they should be "remembered," implicit in his command is the understanding that they should treat the prisoners as they themselves would want to be treated.

Jesus said that He was personally involved in the well-being of such people.

> Then the King will say to those on his right, "Come, you who are blessed by my Father; take your inheritance, the kingdom prepared for you since the creation of the world. For I was hungry and you gave me something to eat, I was thirsty and you gave me something to drink, I was a stranger and you invited me in, I needed clothes and you clothed me, I was sick and you looked after me, I was in prison and you came to visit me." Then the righteous will answer him, "Lord, when did we see you hungry and feed you, or thirsty and give you something to drink? When did we see you a stranger and invite you in, or needing clothes and clothe you? When did we see you sick or in prison and go to visit you?" The King will reply, "I tell you the truth, whatever you did for one of the least of these brothers of mine, you did for me" (Matt. 25:34-40).

In essence this is what He said to Saul of Tarsus on the road to Damascus: "Saul, Saul, why do you persecute me?" (Acts 9:4). Saul was taken aback at the word *me*. He thought he was persecuting heretical Jews, but who was this who said he was being persecuted by Saul? Clearly Jesus takes personally the persecution of His people.

Later in life, Paul wrote, "If one part [one Christian] suffers, every part suffers with it" (1 Cor. 12:26). God expects us to view the problems of others as being our problems. Do you have compassion on those in need? Do you join them under their burden and make them feel, "This is *our* problem"?

Purity — v. 4

Ours is a permissive age, and most of us have lived long enough to see a rapid decline in morality. Explicit sex is commonplace on the movie screen and is beginning to invade TV. Mixed housing at the university openly sanctions pre- and extramarital sex. Homosexuals are campaigning openly for recognition and acceptance. Absolutes have yielded to relativism. The puritan ethic has taken on a negative connotation. For example, a leading sociologist at Arizona State University stated that the "puritanical legal code" has actually *contributed* to the high incidence of crime in the United States.

Truth, however, is not relative, but absolute. Behind the absolute standard of morality that governs our conduct stands the judgment of God. This is the same God whom the author calls "a consuming fire" (Heb. 12:29).

Contentment — vv. 5-6

The apostle Paul said, "The *love* of money is a root of all kinds of evil" (1 Tim. 6:10). Not money, but the *love* of money is the source of many of our problems. This is the point being made here. God, not money, must be the object of our security. To covet money is to expend emotional energy on the wrong thing.

Again the writer brings us back to our concept of God. Contentment is the fruit of believing we are in the center of God's will and that this will is perfect. To support this truth, he quotes from the Old Testament (Deut. 31:6; Josh. 1:5; Ps. 118:6). God is in control of our lives. All that we have is a gift from Him. He gives and withholds on the basis of what is best for us. If we really believe this, we can be content, irrespective of our financial status. Financial gains and losses are not the barometer of the Christian's security; God is.

Faith Expresses Itself in Commitment — *Hebrews 13:7-16*

[7]Remember your leaders, who spoke the word of God to you. Consider the outcome of their way of life and imitate their faith.

[8]Jesus Christ is the same yesterday and today and forever.
[9]Do not be carried away by all kinds of strange teachings. It is good for our hearts to be strengthened by grace, not by ceremonial foods, which are of no value to those who eat them. [10]We have an altar from which those who minister at the tabernacle have no right to eat.
[11]The high priest carries the blood of animals into the Most Holy Place as a sin offering, but the bodies are burned outside the camp. [12]And so Jesus also suffered outside the city gate to make his people holy through his own blood. [13]Let us, then, go to him outside the camp, bearing the disgrace he bore. [14]For here we do not have an enduring city, but we are looking for the city that is to come.
[15]Through Jesus, therefore, let us continually offer to God a sacrifice of praise—the fruit of lips that confess his name. [16]And do not forget to do good and to share with others, for with such sacrifices God is pleased.

Commitment lies at the very heart of faith. Earlier we saw that faith is *commitment before knowledge* (Heb. 11). It is risk-taking. The believer commits himself to what he knows to be God's will and *then* he knows that it was the right thing to do. This is the essence of biblical faith.

Faith finds its expression in commitment, and the writer says we must apply this truth in four areas.

Commitment to Leadership — vv. 7-8

The basis for what he says in this passage is in the statement just before (v. 6). Since God is in control of our destiny, we need not fear what man can do to us. This is why we can submit to spiritual leadership without fear and apprehension.

We must decide before God, however, who our spiritual leaders are to be. God expects all of us to be under authority, but the will of God is different from person to person as to who that authority ought to be. In determining who should rule over us, three questions may be asked.

1. *Do they preach the Word of God?* We cannot tie ourselves to a fellowship that does not honor the Scriptures. If the Bible is used as a tool to justify what is being done, this is not loyalty to the Word. Are the leaders themselves under the authority of the Bible and do they submit to it? This is the first great test.

2. *Do they have faith worth emulating?* William Carey, father of the modern missionary movement, once said, "Expect great things

from God; attempt great things for God.'' Are these leaders actively moving ahead in the known will of God? Are they giving themselves to the Great Commission? Do we sense in the group the excitement of stepping out for God in faith and taking great risks? This is the second great test.

3. *What kind of life are they living?* Are they honest, pure, and sacrificial? Are their family lives worth imitating? Are these leaders living according to the virtues mentioned earlier (vv. 1-6)? This is the third great test.

Once you have determined the will of God in this, then take these people as your God-appointed leaders and follow their example and counsel. Jesus Himself is unchanging (v. 8) and He is in control of our lives. Leaders may veer off course and make mistakes, but they cannot affect us. Our sovereign, unchanging God will see to that.

Commitment to Pure Doctrine — v. 9

Every generation must wrestle afresh with the question of pure doctrine. To the original readers of this letter the question was whether or not it was permissible to eat certain kinds of meat. The biblical thinking and reasoning undergirding this problem had to be resolved.

Philosophically, existentialism today seems to have passed its crest. But it has made a profound impression on society in general and on the church in particular. Its effects will be felt for many years to come. Simply stated, it teaches that there is no personal God controlling the universe. We are locked into a system of chance, from which there is no escape. Life has no meaning, no direction, and no absolutes. In short, all of human life is a ''sick joke.''

Because truth is made relative, it leaves man autonomous. He becomes his own final court of appeal. Significance is measured by that which speaks to him. There is no purpose to life and, therefore, meaning is to be squeezed out of whatever experiences he can have. This in turn irresistably leads to immorality, drugs, and other means that can contribute to obtaining such experiences.

Antiauthoritarianism is one of existentialism's offsprings. ''Since there are no absolutes and I am my own judge, don't tell me what to do'' is one of its dictums. Biblical authority and the inspiration of the Bible are questioned and the church is forced to wrestle with this doctrine.

The distinctive role and function of the sexes is rooted in a theistic concept of absolutes. Because this is denied today, the emphasis is placed on unisex and an "equal" role for women—"equal" here meaning "the same as" the man. So men wear long hair and carry purses, and women wear neckties. "Women's liberation" is a movement that grows in influence and all forms of opposition are labeled "male chauvinism." Women are admitted into roles of authority in the church against the express command of Scripture and this is excused by suggesting that such commands are no longer "authoritative" for us today.

All of this is illustrative of the fact that the church is faced with the necessary task of seeking to keep her doctrine pure. This responsibility, however, must be predicated on the assumption that true faith properly expresses itself in a commitment to pure doctrine and that for doctrine to be pure it must be derived from the Bible alone.

Commitment to Christ's Rejection — vv. 10-14

In making this poignant application, the writer returns to the sacrificial system described in the Old Testament (see Lev. 16). On the Day of Atonement, the high priest first offered a bull for his own sins; the animal was sacrificed on the brazen altar and the blood taken by the high priest into the Holy of Holies and sprinkled on the mercy seat.

Next, the high priest took one of two goats and did the same with it, this time sacrificing for the sins of the people. He then laid his hands on the second living goat, the "scape-goat," and confessed over it all the iniquities of the people. "The goat will carry on itself all their sins to a solitary place; and the man shall release it in the desert" (Lev. 16:22).

The final act in this drama was when the carcases of the bull and the first goat were taken outside the camp to a clean place and burned. "The bull and the goat for the sin offerings, whose blood was brought into the Most Holy Place to make atonement, must be taken outside the camp; and their hides, flesh and offal are to be burned up" (Lev. 16:27).

True to this pattern, says the writer, Jesus was similarly taken outside the gate to suffer and be rejected (Heb. 13:12). His blood was brought into the very presence of God where propitiation for sin was made, but His body was taken outside the city to a place of rejection, just like the bull and goat in Leviticus 16.

Then we are told that commitment means that we too must follow Jesus "outside the city gate" (Heb. 13:13). Earlier we were told that we join Christ in the holy presence of God and are washed from our sins. Just as Jesus followed the Old Testament pattern of going into the Holy of Holies and we followed Him there for atonement, so also Jesus followed the Old Testament pattern of suffering outside the camp, and we are to follow Him there to the place of rejection.

All of us are enthralled by the thought of joining Jesus in the Holy of Holies, but the thought of joining Him on the cross has little appeal. What does it mean to bear His disgrace? For the original recipients of this letter, it meant being called to suffer persecution for their faith.

The letter now comes full circle to the place where it began—an appeal not to reject Christ and return to Moses in the face of adversity. Christianity is a package deal. To accept His sacrifice for sin is to accept a share in His rejection. So we are urged, "Let us then approach the throne of grace" (Heb. 4:16), and, "Let us, then, go to Him outside the camp" (Heb. 13:13).

For most of us in the western world the kind of persecution for the faith experienced by these early believers is totally alien. Adversity, however, strikes the lives of all of us, but the forms it takes may be different. Just prior to His ascension, Jesus was talking to Peter.

> "Feed my sheep. [18]I tell you the truth, when you were younger you dressed yourself and went where you wanted; but when you are old you will stretch out your hands, and someone else will dress you and lead you where you do not want to go." [19]Jesus said this to indicate the kind of death by which Peter would glorify God. Then he said to him, "Follow me!"
>
> [20]Peter turned and saw that the disciple whom Jesus loved was following them. (This was the one who had leaned back against Jesus at the supper and had said, "Lord, who is going to betray you?"). [21]When Peter saw him, he asked, "Lord, what about him?"
>
> [22]Jesus answered, "If I want him to remain alive until I return, what is that to you? You must follow me" (John 21:18-22).

Commitment to Christ's rejection means a willingness to take God's path for your life irrespective of where that path may lead.

Commitment to Good Works — vv. 15-16

The day of sacrificing animals has passed. But there are other kinds of sacrifices the committed Christian can offer to delight the heart of God. Three such sacrifices are suggested to us.

1. *Continual praise and thanksgiving to God* (v. 15). Most of us are weak in our expressions of praise. The Lord desires that we have thankful hearts, and express them to Him. David was "a man after God's own heart," and when we read the psalms with their continual

praise to God, it is easy to see why. Make a habit of regularly worshiping the Lord with praise and thanksgiving.

2. *Good deeds* (v. 16a). Look for opportunities to do good to others. Ask the Lord to give you eyes to see other people's needs. Bob Pierce, founder of World Vision, prayed, "Lord break my heart with the things that break Your heart." See the world through the eyes of Jesus, and yours will be a life filled with doing good. This is a sacrifice well pleasing to God.

3. *Share with others* (v. 16b). This means being generous. God loves generous people. The reason why this is such an important ingredient in the Christian life probably lies in the fact that Jesus Himself is generous. God is a giving God, and to give is to be Godlike. When we see a generous Christian, we see one who is moving ahead in the Christian life. When we see a person who is not generous, no matter what else he may be doing in the Christian life, we see a person who is stagnating.

When we combine these four applications of what it means to be committed to the life of faith—following our leaders, embracing pure doctrine, joining Jesus in His rejection, and doing good works—with *virtuous conduct* (vv. 1-6), we begin to have a comprehensive, well-rounded picture of the Christian life.

Faith Expresses Itself in Obedience — *Hebrews 13:17-25*

[17]Obey your leaders and submit to their authority. They keep watch over you as men who must give an account. Obey them so that their work will be a joy, not a burden, for that would be of no advantage to you.

[18]Pray for us. We are sure that we have a clear conscience and desire to live honorably in every way. [19]I particularly urge you to pray so that I may be restored to you soon.

[20]May the God of peace, who through the blood of the eternal covenant brought back from the dead our Lord Jesus, that great Shepherd of the sheep, [21]equip you with everything good for doing his will, and may he work in us what is pleasing to him, through Jesus Christ, to whom be glory for ever and ever. Amen.

[22]Brothers, I urge you to bear with my word of exhortation, for I have written you only a short letter.

[23]I want you to know that our brother Timothy has been released. If he arrives soon, I will come with him to see you.

[24]Greet all your leaders and all God's people. Those from Italy send you their greetings.

[25]Grace be with you all.

We come now to the end of the Epistle to the Hebrews. A few instructions and closing comments remain before the writer concludes with a benediction for God's grace to rest on his readers. But even in these random thoughts we can see the desire of his heart summarized: that we be obedient to others, to Christ, and to the Word.

Obedience to Leadership — vv. 17-19

I was having lunch with a friend one day and during our conversation he asked if I could join him on a particular trip. I replied that I would be delighted to, but that I would first have to check with my leaders in The Navigators. This opened up a Pandora's box as he expressed in no uncertain terms his disapproval at a grown man having to do this. He pitied me. To him, the idea of being in submission to another was unthinkable.

I asked him, "Who watches for your soul as they that must give an account? Who loves you and has your best interest at heart? Who prays for you and counsels you objectively, seeking God's best for you?"

"No one," he replied.

"Then don't pity me for being under the authority of another," I stated. "You are the one to be pitied, not I. The men who watch for my soul are among the greatest heritages I have in the world. I am to be envied, not pitied."

Obedience to Christ — vv. 20-21

This great benediction suggests that He who has saved us is continuing His work in us, making us sensitive to His will so that all we do is pleasing in His sight. Obedience to Jesus Christ is first and foremost in the Christian life. The truest expression of faith is obedience to the Godhead.

Obedience to the Word — vv. 22-25

The writer exhorts, "Suffer the Word." "Bear patiently with me," he pleads, "as I share the Word with you. Patiently take it in and digest it, for the letter isn't all that long." When God speaks, as He has done in this book, we must listen and apply what we have heard.

This is a fitting summary for the entire book: obey Jesus Christ, obey the Bible, and obey those God has put over us. That—as our unsurpassed, incomparable way of life *after the sacrifice*—is superior living!